Vegetable Gardening & Cooking

BY DOROTHY and THOMAS HOOBLER

GROSSET
GOOD LIFE
BOOKS

PUBLISHERS • GROSSET & DUNLAP • NEW YORK
A FILMWAYS COMPANY

Acknowledgments

Produced for Grosset & Dunlap by Media Projects Inc., New York, N.Y.

Cover photograph by Tony Gauba (Freelance Photographers Guild, Inc.)
All illustrations by Abe Echevarria

Photographs by: Elinor S. Beckwith, pages 4, 26, 30, 36, 37, 38, 39, 42, 44, 48, 58, 59, 63, 67, and 83; J. C. Penney Co., pages 32-33; W. Atlee Burpee Co., pages 40, 64, 65 (top and bottom), and 79; Ferry-Morse Seed Co., page 65 (center); U. S. Department of Agriculture, page 76.

Instructions for recipes and safety precautions in this book are in accord with the standards of the U.S. Department of Agriculture and have been carefully checked for accuracy. However, the author and publisher do not warrant or guarantee results and cannot be responsible for any adverse consequences resulting from the use of information contained herein. The author has attempted to assist the reader in avoiding problems by setting forth appropriate and recommended procedures.

1976 PRINTING

Contents

1
Garden Basics

This book is for those who are setting out to grow food for their families in their own backyard. Anyone who has access to even a small plot of land can plant a garden for food, and anyone who is willing to learn the basics of preserving food can reap the goodness — and the economy — of home-grown fruits and vegetables all through the year.

Growing food on your own land is not an idea that began in the twentieth century. Complicated and expensive equipment, fertilizers, and chemicals were not needed by our forebears to subsist off the land — they are the tools of farmers, not gardeners. For you, the gardener, there need be no mystique about growing plants. Nature does the really important work for you.

The methods outlined in this book are elementary but complete. You will need no further instruction, though there are many worthwhile publications and books that will broaden your knowledge of how to help things grow. The important thing to remember about gardening is that it can be simple. We try to show you how your garden can be maintained with as little time and trouble as possible — certainly no more than the weekend gardener can manage.

For each crop we have included basic recipes and methods for canning, freezing, or storing food. We felt these would be helpful to you if you are setting out to fill, or help fill, family food needs from your own yard.

As we prepared this book, we wanted to include an estimate of how much you can save by growing the vegetables suggested on a 20 by 30 foot plot of land. We realized, however, that it is impossible to predict the prices of food even next month, much less those of a year or more away. Pages 14 and 15, however, show you how to figure out the economics based on local costs. As prices rise, and shortages increase, growing your own food becomes more and more attractive. We are realizing in America that our days of profligate waste are over, and one of our biggest areas of waste lies right in our own yards — valuable space used for growing only grass.

Go out and walk in your yard. Turn over a shovelful of soil. Feel it with your bare hands and see how good the feeling is. That soil is good for something.

The Garden Plan

The garden here, and the graph paper plan of it on the next page, is scaled to 20 by 30 feet. It is large enough to provide most of the fresh and preserved produce for an average family, but small enough for the weekend gardener to keep up. It includes the following fruits and vegetables:

apples
asparagus
beans
beets
cabbage
carrots
corn
cucumbers
eggplant
grapes
herbs
lettuce
parsnips
pears
peas
peppers
tomatoes
turnips
salsify
strawberries

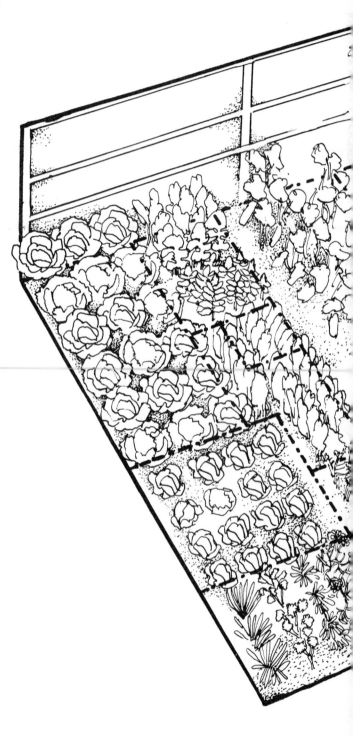

The plan is to a large extent based on getting the most food, in the least space, especially those crops that are best for storage and preserving. Therefore little room is given to corn, because its yield is small in relation to the space it needs to grow, but plenty is given to tomatoes and to cucumbers, which both produce heavily and have excellent preserving qualities.

In other words, this plan has an economic bias; feel free to throw thrift to the winds, and plant only what you like best to eat.

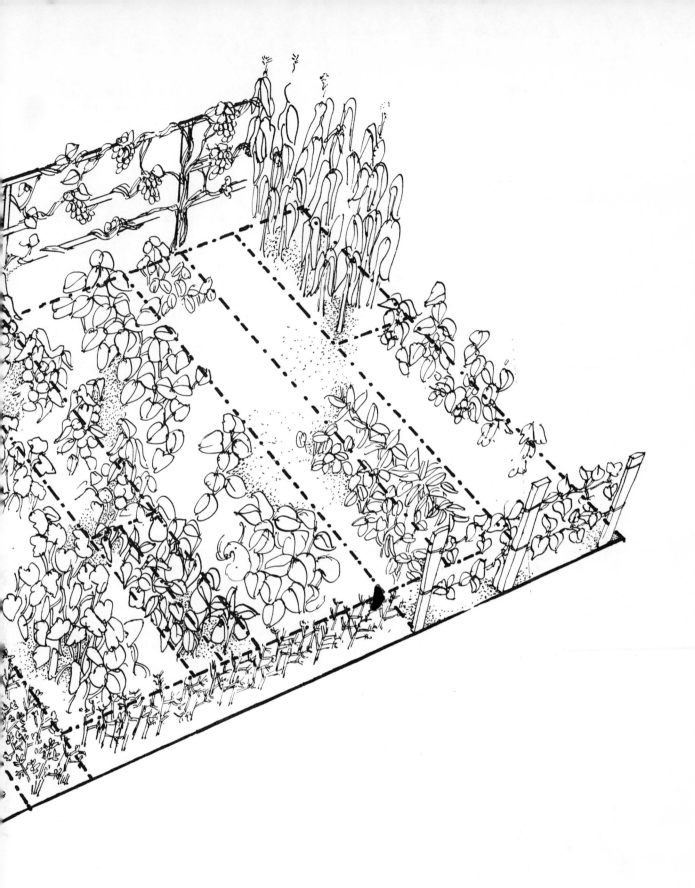

By using graph paper to plan your garden, you can easily see how much space you will need to get the amount of produce you want from each crop. This plan shows the 20 by 30 foot garden on the preceding page. Where possible, we have indicated the actual number of plants in each area based on the suggested distance between plants and between rows. Using the estimating chart on pages 12 and 13, you can figure out about how many cabbages, or how much eggplant you might produce, and increase or decrease an area accordingly. This size graph paper is called ¼ inch, which means it is divided into ¼-inch squares. We have drawn the plan so that each ¼ inch equals 1 foot of garden. You can use an ordinary ruler and count up the quarters to measure the length of a row, or the distance between rows.

Some of the vegetables can be planted either in hills (groups) or drills (rows). We have indicated cucumbers, squash and corn as being planted in hills.

Radishes can be planted among the other root crops, or in any of the spaces between some of the larger vegetables, so they have no specific spot of their own.

At the bottom of the plan, we have indicated both cabbage and lettuce in the same area. Lettuce can be planted between the cabbage plants, grown to maturity and harvested before the cabbage grows large enough to need the space. This interplanting method can be used with other vegetables as well. Squash, for instance, can be interplanted with quick-maturing root crops or herbs. Use your own space the way you think best. Don't be afraid to experiment.

N

North is indicated on the plan to help you orient your own garden. The direction of the rows follows the east to west path of the sun. Tall plants such as corn are planted at the north end of the garden so they don't shade out the shorter plants.

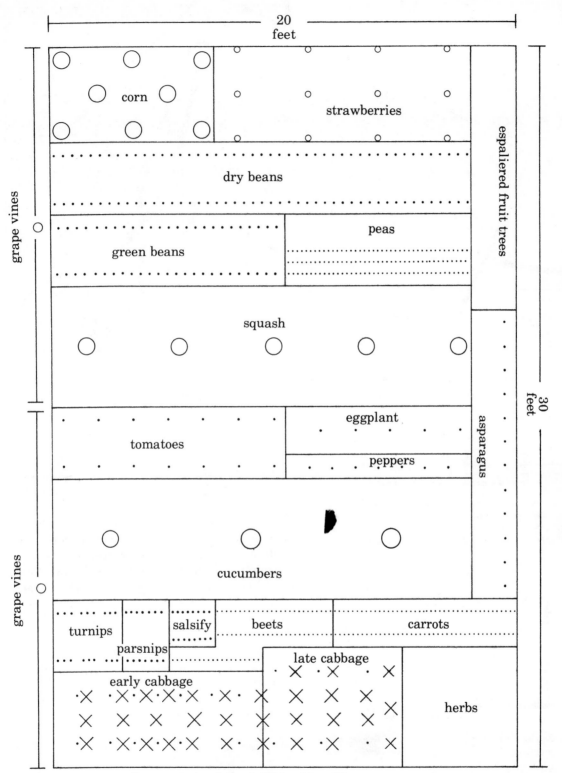

20 feet

30 feet

grape vines

corn

strawberries

dry beans

green beans

peas

squash

tomatoes

eggplant

peppers

asparagus

espaliered fruit trees

cucumbers

turnips

salsify

beets

carrots

parsnips

late cabbage

early cabbage

herbs

lettuce interplanted (X's) with cabbage

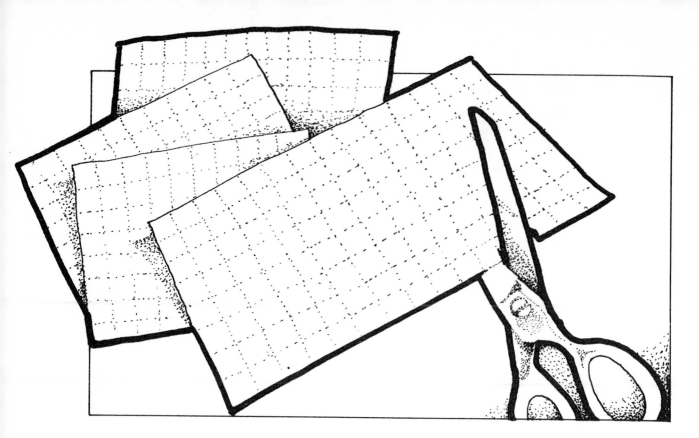

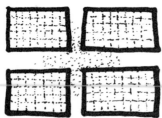

The first step in planning is to cut pieces of graph paper to the approximate sizes you think you need for each crop. Cut or tape on more paper as you determine the final shape of each segment. Don't forget to label the name of the crop.

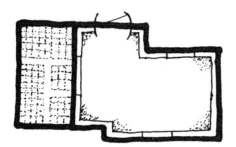

This is the plan for a small garden tucked in where one wing of the house forms an interior, sunny corner with the main house. It is large enough for tomatoes, salad greens and herbs, the produce a good cook might want close to his or her kitchen door.

How To Use The Plan

We know there are many people who will go out in the spring, plant seeds wherever they feel the urge, and happily harvest as the seeds grow into mature plants. They don't need charts, plans or guides, and feel constricted by them.

There is pleasure, however, in planning. Few people will want to plan for exactly the garden here. You may not have this much land available for planting; or if you do, perhaps it is under a big maple tree, or just where the family plays badminton. But there is no rule that says a garden has to be a rectangle in the middle of your lawn. Walk around your property — could you plant tomatoes, salad greens and peppers along the south or west wall of your house? Perhaps a garden would fit along the fence at your boundary, or on both sides of a path. You may find other spots where you can tuck in some plants — pole beans among flowers, for instance; a pretty pea border that is pulled out after early harvest and replaced with marigolds; herbs at the edge of a foundation planting; a row of corn behind the garage. Measure the likely spots, and get out your graph paper and a pair of scissors. Draw squares or rectangles to represent the places you have found, and match them up with the crops you would like to grow.

Another problem may be a reluctance to turn a section of a beautifully landscaped yard into a vegetable garden. We can only suggest that if you have had the skill to landscape a yard, you will have the skill to design a handsome vegetable garden. Again, cut the graph paper into segments for each crop, and then begin to arrange and rearrange them until some pattern catches your eye. Try quadrants divided by grass paths, or long strips of vegetables (they can be curved strips too) or square plots arranged in a pleasing pattern. When you are on the track of a design you like, cut down or add to each segment to get it the right size and shape to fit your plan.

Your choice of vegetables and fruits may be limited by extremes of climate. You may live too far north to plant eggplant, or too far south for apples. Look under "cultivation" for those crops that interest you, and see when to plant, how long it requires from planting to harvesting, and whether harvesting must be done before the first frost. Then refer to the zone map on pages 16 and 17 to see if the dates of last frost in your area will give enough time for the crops you have in mind.

Then there are problems of preference and of economics. Poll your family for their tastes; you will not be happy with your crop of 210 cucumbers if all the children say "yuck" to pickles; so plan your yields accordingly by using the yield chart on the next page. As for the economics, use the yield chart to calculate what you can expect to harvest, then use the cost chart on pages 14 and 15 to figure what a garden will cost you to grow. A little more arithmetic, using local produce prices, will tell you how much you might save. Many of you will find green thumbs sprouting where only an opposable digit grew before, and thus that the estimated yields were too low. Now you know the joy of a farmer in a good year.

Farmers live in bad times too, and the perils of insects, blight, birds, wind, rain, no rain, and just bad ground lie in wait. If your garden doesn't work out, you'll have to look for the pioneer spirit to start again, this year or next. We hope you find that it's still there.

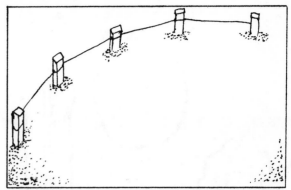

To lay out a curved garden, put in stakes every few feet and tie string between them to mark the curve before you hoe the drills.

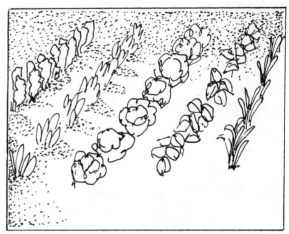

A garden formed of narrow strips separated by grass paths is more difficult to set up, but is easy to weed and cultivate. You can water it when you water your lawn.

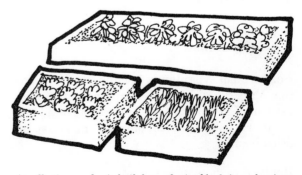

An effective garden is built here of raised beds in a pleasing pattern.

Yield Chart

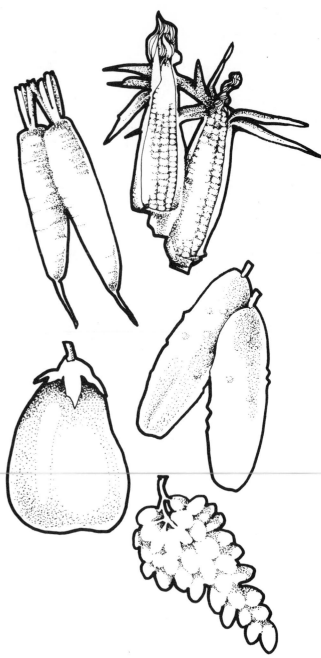

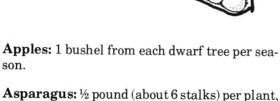

Apples: 1 bushel from each dwarf tree per season.

Asparagus: ½ pound (about 6 stalks) per plant, or per foot of row.

Beans: bush type plants, 1 pound to each foot of row. Vine types, 2 pounds per plant or 4 pounds per foot of row if harvested green; ½ pound per plant or 1 pound per foot of row if harvested as dried beans.

Beets: 6 roots to each foot of row.

Cabbage: 3 pounds (about 2 heads of large, late variety) per each foot of row.

Carrots: 6 roots of the larger varieties, or 8 roots of the smaller varieties for each foot of row.

Corn: 1 to 3 ears per plant, or about 5 ears to a hill of 3 plants.

Cucumbers: about 70 cucumbers for each hill of 3 plants.

Eggplant: about 4 fruits per plant, or 1½ eggplants for each foot of row.

Grapes: between 10 and 20 pounds from each mature vine.

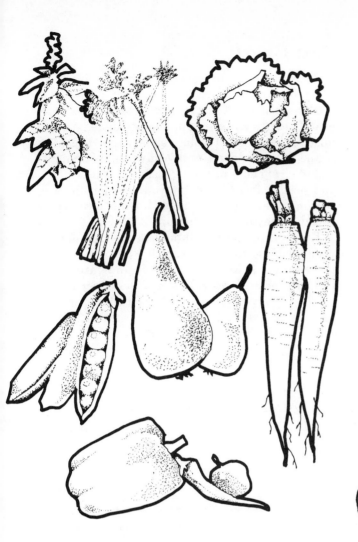
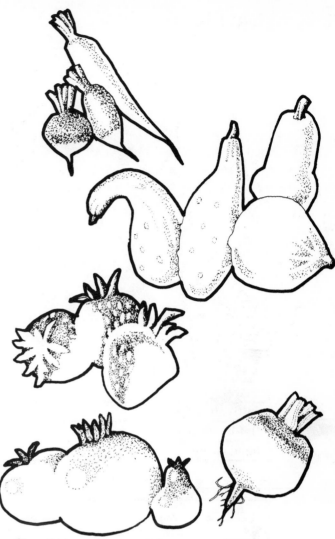

Herbs: In general, a family of four will obtain sufficient herbs from 3 basil plants, 3 chives, 6 parsley, 3 mint, 2 dill, 1 sage, 1 oregano, 1 rosemary and 1 tarragon.

Lettuce: 1 head for each foot of row.

Parsnips: 4 roots for each foot of row.

Pears: 1 bushel from each dwarf tree per season.

Peas: pole type, 1 pound from each plant or nearly 10 pounds for each foot of row. Bush type, 1/3 pound from each plant, or 3 pounds for each foot of row.

Peppers: about ½ pound (30 small chili peppers, 6 bell peppers) from each plant, or from 2½ to 3 pounds for each foot of row.

Radishes: 8 to 12 roots for each foot of row.

Salsify: 4 roots for each foot of row.

Squash: summer varieties, 10 pounds (about 10 young fruits) from each plant, or 30 pounds per hill of 3 plants. Winter varieties, from 10 to 30 pounds (2 to 8 fruits), depending on variety, from each plant, or 30 to 90 pounds per hill of 3 plants.

Strawberries: 1 pint berries from each plant, or nearly a pint for each foot of row.

Tomatoes: bush type, 8 pounds (35 plum tomatoes, 10 beefsteak tomatoes) per plant, or about 6 pounds for each foot of row. Vine type, same yield as bush type if staked; if unstaked and allowed to grow along the ground for full length, 15 pounds (40 plum tomatoes, 15 beefsteak tomatoes) per plant, or 5 pounds for each foot of row.

Turnips: 2 to 5 turnips, depending on size of variety, for each foot of row.

Cost Chart

Before you start to scare yourself by filling in every item on these charts, ask yourself what you really need. You probably already have a hose, lawn sprinkler and hand-spade. You might like to start your cabbages in a cold frame, but you don't really have to. Wait for trouble from dogs or rabbits before you assume you need a fence. And try your garden for a season in the soil you already have before you spend money on extra topsoil.

The costs are divided into those that are one-time (or close to it — you will wear out your gloves after a while), and those that are repeated year after year, like seed, fertilizer and twine. We have left several lines for what might need to be itemized. For instance, seeds of different kinds, or cold frame materials.

Start-up Costs

shovel	
cultivating hoe	
flat-blade hoe	
hand spade	
gloves	
wheelbarrow	
hose	
sprinkler	
sprayer	
topsoil	
fence	
cold frame	
lumber for raised beds	
flats for starting seeds	
reusable pots (clay or plastic)	
grape vines	
dwarf fruit trees	

Annual Costs

seed	
plants	
potting soil	
consumable pots (peat pots or pellets)	
Hot-Kaps or similar weather guards	
mulching materials	
fertilizer	
insecticide	
wire mesh for training plants	
stakes and poles	
ties and/or twine	

Zone Map

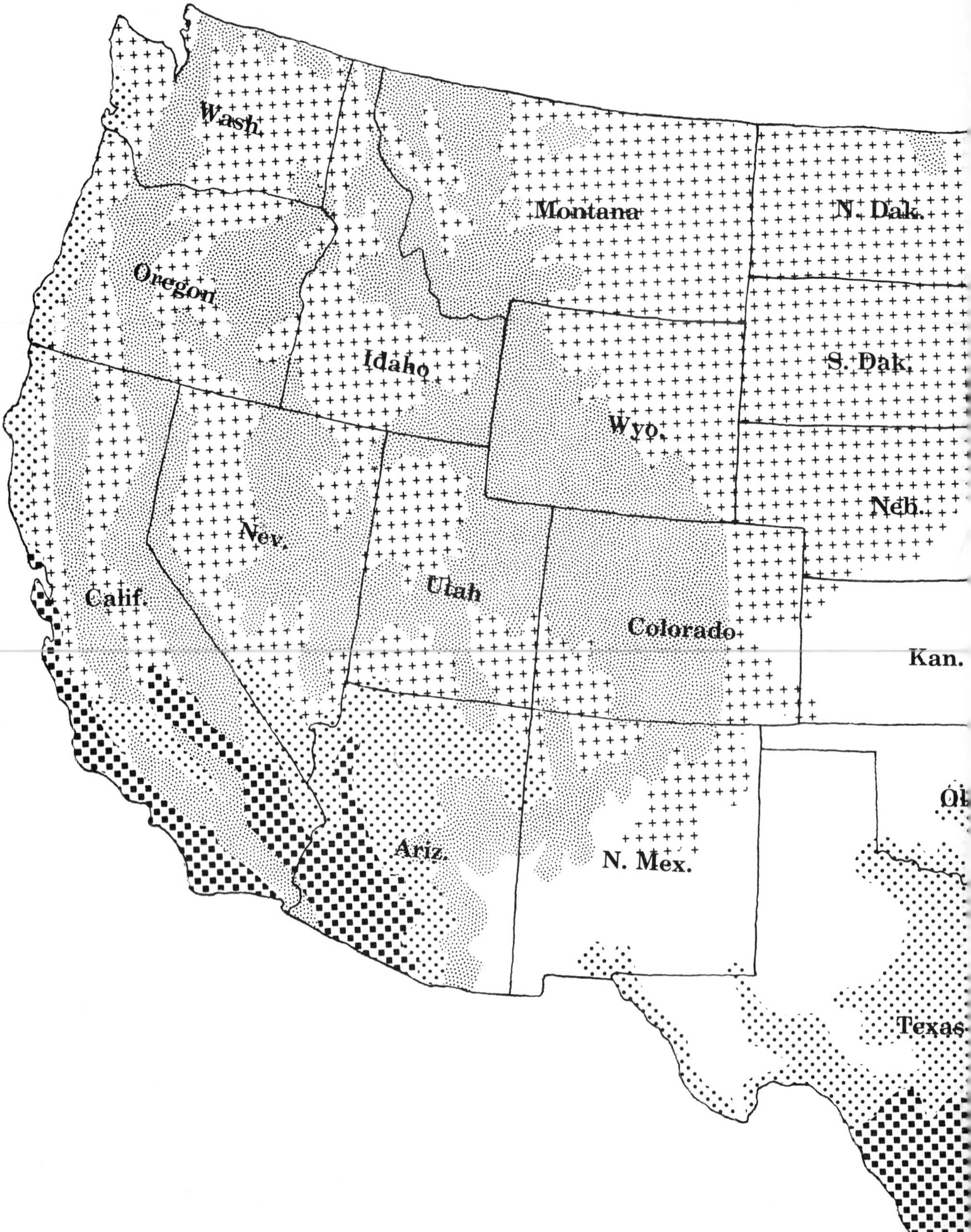

Wash.

Oregon

Idaho

Montana

N. Dak.

S. Dak.

Wyo.

Nev.

Utah

Colorado

Neb.

Kan.

Calif.

Ariz.

N. Mex.

Ok.

Texas

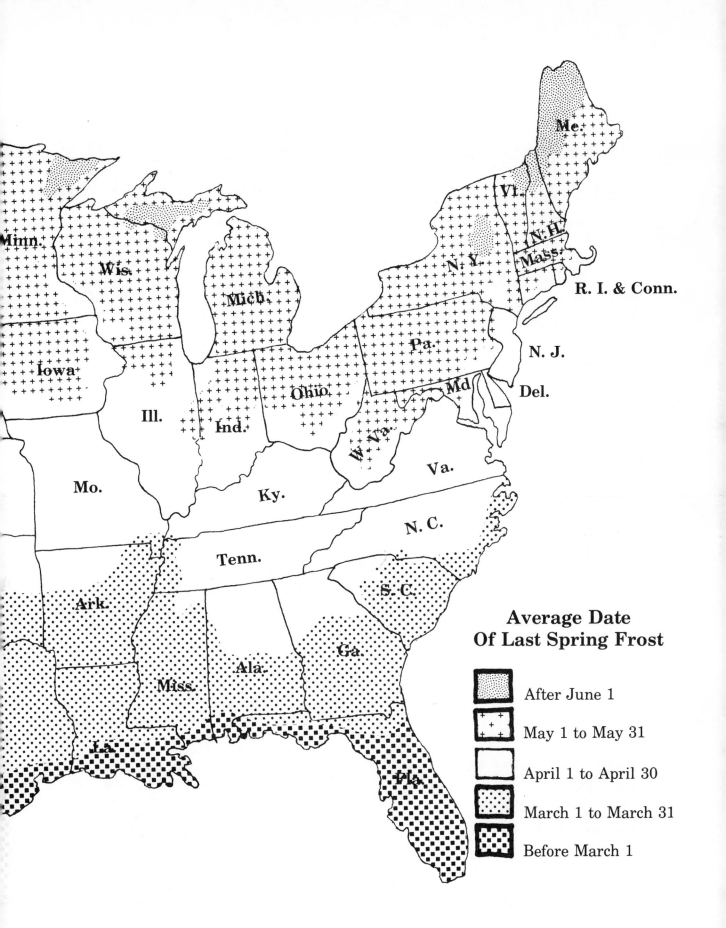

**Average Date
Of Last Spring Frost**

After June 1

May 1 to May 31

April 1 to April 30

March 1 to March 31

Before March 1

Choosing A Location

The first thing you have to do to start a garden is find a good place for it. The two essentials you will be looking for are drainage and light. You don't want to plant in a sunken area that collects water after a storm because that will harm vegetable roots. And don't plant in a spot that will be shaded by your house or trees; a vegetable garden needs at least five hours of sun a day.

Plant your garden on level ground, if you can. If you have no level spot, growing a garden on a hill, though harder on you, isn't impossible.

Preparing The Ground

Clearing the ground to be planted is your first gardening job. Mark the area with a stake at each corner, with twine tied between the stakes so you can see where your edges are. Remove the turf, if the area has been lawn.

Turn over the top 6 to 8 inches of soil with a shovel, breaking up tightly packed ground with a hoe and removing stones, large twigs and so on.

If this is your first garden, it is a good idea to evaluate your soil.

Soil

Soil Texture

Soil is made up of sand, clay and humus. Humus is decayed vegetable matter. More than that, humus is the part of your soil that holds water and keeps it handy for plants to use. Humus, unlike clay, doesn't pack hard when it dries out. Rather, it looks dark and crumbly. The chief sources of humus are compost and the manure of vegetable-eating animals, such as cows, horses and chickens.

Both manure and compost also supply some nutrients to the soil and are often used as fertilizers. You can never have too much humus.

You can, however, have too much clay or too much sand. Pick up a nice moist handful of your garden soil. When you open your hand, does it hold together in a ball? If it doesn't, your soil is too sandy. If it does, poke it with your finger and drop the ball on the ground. If it doesn't break

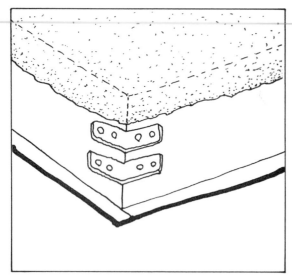

Raised beds are a good solution if your soil is not good for garden vegetables. Make a box frame (or several frames) of 2 foot x 10 foot cedar or redwood, or pine painted with creosote to prevent rotting. Strengthen the corner joints with angle irons. Pack the frame with good topsoil (look in local newspapers for topsoil offers). Soil is sold by the cubic yard. One yard covers an area 6 feet by 6 feet by 9 inches deep.

apart now, your soil is mostly clay — which means it won't drain well and will pack hard when it dries, stopping plant growth. Both too sandy or too clayey means bad news for your plants.

If you decide you have a soil problem, you'll have to add some of the missing ingredients to a depth of 8 to 10 inches to balance things out. This is a big job, and can be made easier by using a Rotovator, or power cultivator. You might be able to rent one at a garden center or rent-all outlet. Add sharp sand and humus to clayey soil until it is more friable. Add humus to sandy soil until it holds together better. There is no way to predict exact quantities, so you will have to be the judge.

If you plant your garden on the side of a hill, make the rows along the side of the hill – not up and down. The contours prevent erosion, and ensure more even distribution of water. Plant root crops at top, and vine crops at the bottom.

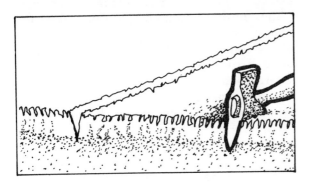

To de-turf, cut the grass layer into strips 18 inches wide and 3 inches deep with an axe.

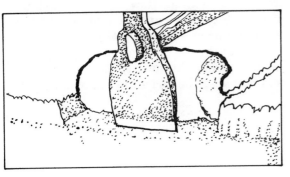

The grass roots must be broken through with a grub hoe as the strips of turf are rolled up. The rolled-up turf can be used to replace bare spots in your lawn.

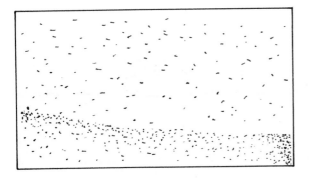

With a hoe, chop up and hoe under all remaining roots of grass and weeds, so that a bare and fertile patch of earth remains.

Soil Acidity

The pH of soil is a measurement of how acid or alkaline your garden soil is. A reading of 7.0 is neither acid nor alkaline. Higher than that is alkaline, lower is acid. All of the plants in this book will thrive with slightly acid soil — 6.0 to 7.0. And good news: If this is your first attempt at planting a garden, your soil is likely to be slightly acid.

After a couple of years of gardening on the same spot, the open soil will tend to become too acid because calcium in the form of lime will have washed away. It must be replaced, or your plants will produce less. Dolomite limestone, purchased at garden supply outlets, should be worked into the soil. Sparingly, please. Use about 5 pounds for every 100 square feet of soil.

The unusual condition of a soil that is too alkaline (much above 7.5) can be corrected by adding sulphur in the form of ammonium sulphate at the rate of 2½ pounds for every 100 square feet of soil. Correcting soil to change pH should be done in the fall, if possible, to give the chemicals time to leach through the soil evenly.

Soil Fertilization

Plants absorb their food from materials in your soil. These materials must be replenished from time to time. How that replenishment should be carried out is a matter of intense dispute among gardeners. Organic gardeners insist that the use of chemical fertilizers is unhealthy and has harmful effects on soil, plants, and humans. The "scientific" gardeners, advo-

To build a compost heap, choose a shady spot near a source of water. In the spring, clear the area to bare ground. Then pile up 6 inches of organic matter like grass clippings, dead leaves, or dampened newspapers. A compost heap is not boxed in. (Ours is shown small for clarity.)

Add layers of garden soil, manure, and organic matter (like vegetable and fruit peels and scraps, coffee grounds, weeds, grass clippings and leaves) as often as you accumulate materials. Keep the pile damp by adding water.

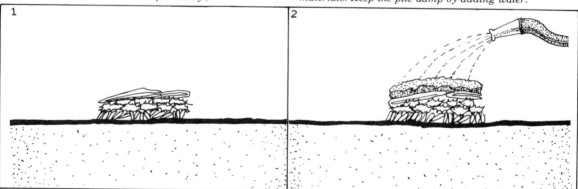

cates of chemical fertilizers, stress the safety, effectiveness, and convenience of chemicals.

Most responsible authorities admit that overuse of chemical fertilizers can damage the physical properties of your soil. This is particularly true if the same type of chemical fertilizer is used for several seasons. It seems to us that the responsible and prudent course is to use natural fertilizers wherever possible.

The three most important components of fertilizer are nitrogen, phosphoric acid and potash. The three numbers you see on packaged fertilizer of all kinds refer to these three components. A package labeled "4-8-4," for example, has 4% nitrogen, 8% phosphoric acid, and 4% potash in its contents. The remainder is inert material.

A 25-pound bag of the well balanced general purpose 10-10-10 fertilizer will be enough to start the garden described in this book (600 square feet). If you have a different-sized garden, figure on using about 4 pounds of 10-10-10 fertilizer for each 100 square feet. Fertilize in the spring after the ground has thawed, digging the fertilizer well into the soil; or in the fall after your crops have been harvested.

Good commercial organic fertilizers are blood meal (nitrogen) and bone meal (nitrogen and phosphorus). If bone meal is used alone, use about 2½ pounds for each 100 square feet. If you use both together, 10 ounces of blood meal and 12 ounces of bone meal per 100 square feet is enough.

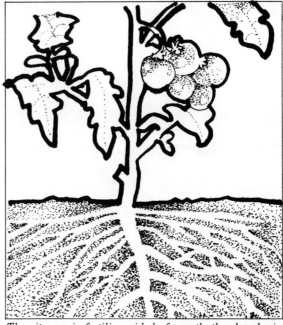

The nitrogen in fertilizer aids leaf growth, the phosphoric acid encourages flower (and hence fruit) growth, and the potash stimulates root growth. For the typical garden which includes leafy, flowering, and root crops, your best bet is an all-purpose fertilizer with an equal balance of the three elements. A balance such as 10-10-10 is good.

Wood ashes, 14 ounces per 100 square feet, are an organic source for potash. Seaweed or fish scraps are also potash sources. Two pounds of these for every 100 square feet of garden will suffice. Compost can also be used as a mild fertilizer, in a ratio of 100 pounds to 100 square feet of soil.

Turn the pile with a garden fork twice a month so the newer layers are turned to the inside, the older layers to the outside. As the pile begins to decompose, it will become quite warm – a sign that everything is working.

By the end of August, stop adding new material, but continue to turn and dampen until first frost. Meanwhile, start a new compost heap next to the older one. In the spring, dig the dark, nicely decayed old compost into the garden. The new heap will be ready the following spring.

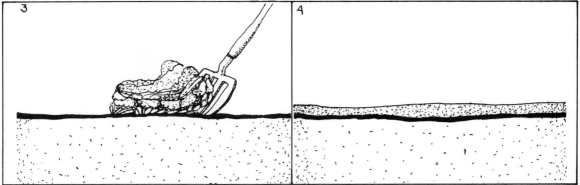

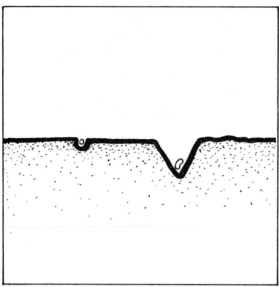

The depth of a drill depends, in general, on the size of the seed you are planting. A shallow drill for small seeds like lettuce is made by pulling your finger along the row. A deep drill or trench, for large seeds like beans, is made by pulling a hoe through the soil.

Planting

Some of the plants in your garden can be started from seed indoors, when the ground outside is still frozen. Others can only be started outside when the ground and weather are suitable. If you're in no hurry, or if the gardening season in your area is long, you can start all the plants from seed outside. This is the easiest way, since it avoids transplanting. Certain vegetables, like tomatoes and eggplant, are available at garden stores as young plants ready for transplanting.

Planting Outdoors

When you are convinced that winter is over and the last frost has come and gone, and when you have finished preparing the soil in your garden, it is time to begin your outdoor planting.

Water the ground lightly beforehand. If you water after planting, you can wash the seeds away.

Instructions on how deep to plant each seed, how close together, and how to space the rows, will be found on your seed packets or in the Fruits And Vegetables section of this book. The two possible ways to plant are referred to as "drills" and "hills."

"Planting in drills" means to plant in a row, or a trench. Deep trenches, of 3 or 4 inches, are made with a hoe; shallow trenches are usually made with a finger.

"Planting in hills" doesn't mean on a mound, but rather in a circle of 4, 5, 6 or more equally spaced seeds. Sometimes the area of the circle will be prepared with extra fertilizer. With certain plants, the earth is built up in the circle after the seeds sprout — hence the name "hill."

Planting Indoors

If you have the room and the urge, starting some of your plants indoors in the wintertime can give you a head start toward the harvest. If the growing season is short in your area, starting seeds indoors may be a necessity if you are to harvest certain crops at all. Tomatoes, cabbage, and summer squash are three suitable plants.

Indoors, seeds are started in containers. There's no formality about containers — anything from paper cups to specially-built flats will work. All that is necessary is that they hold deep enough soil (3 inches will do nicely) and can sit in front of a sunny window for a month or two. You can supply drainage by poking holes in the bottom of the container and having another container underneath to catch the water.

Actually, you can use containers with closed bottoms if the drainage problem is liable to ruin someone's prized table or rug. Just restrain yourself from overwatering. Always let the soil get barely dry before rewatering.

About that soil — it's better not to take a handful from the garden to start seedlings indoors. You should use a special "medium," like peat moss, vermiculite, or sand, or a mixture of the three. The seed starting mixes you buy at your local garden store are sterilized and will give your seedlings a good start in life.

If you're using containers without drainage, you can save yourself from overwatering until the seeds sprout by a simple method. After you plant the seeds and water for the first time, cover the top of the container with a sheet of plastic or small clear plastic bags. Do not water again until the seeds sprout. The plastic will keep the moisture from escaping.

Plant seeds inside at the same depths recommended on the package for each crop or in the Fruits And Vegetables section of this book.

When the first green shoots appear, remove the plastic if you have used it. But don't water a second time until the soil is barely dry.

From then on, good light is the most important need. If you have your plants in a very hot window, with direct sun, the plants may begin to wilt or burn. If so, draw the blinds or move the plants on the sunniest days.

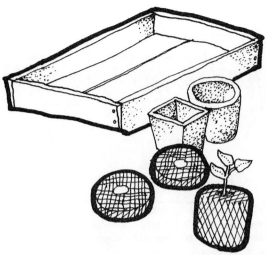

A flat is a wood or plastic box in which quite a few plants can be started. Plastic pots or paper cups can be used too. But the easiest way to start seed is in peat pots or peat pellets, both of which can be placed directly into the garden later without removing the baby plant from its container.

Mark your garden by driving some temporary stakes in the ground on both sides of the garden at the distances between rows recommended under "cultivation" for each crop. Stretch strings across to mark the rows. Planting in straight rows won't help the plants grow, but it will save precious space and help you tell the vegetables from the weeds when both sprout together.

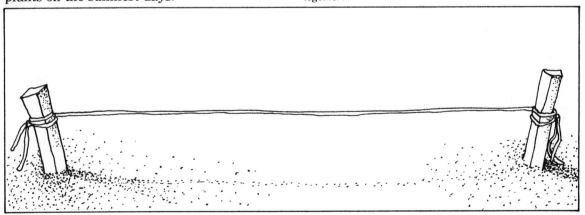

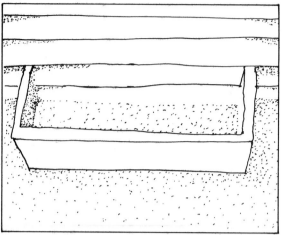

A cold frame can easily be built by making a rectangle of cement blocks or 2 foot x 10 foot cedar, redwood, or creosote-painted pine against a sunny wall of a house or warm building.

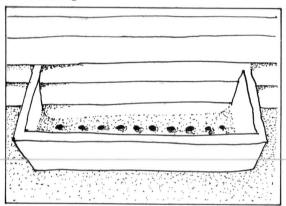

The interior of the frame can be dug out to give more depth for growing seedlings. The soil should be about 8 inches deep, and of the same quality as the garden, unless you are using the cold frame only as a receptacle for plants in pots.

A clear top must be provided, with provision for opening to permit air circulation on hot days. An old storm door will serve, as will plastic stretched across a wooden frame. The top is propped open when necessary with a stick.

Thinning Seedlings

More seeds will sprout, whether you planted indoors or out, than you have room for. The seedlings will have to be thinned. If you don't thin, your garden will become crowded with small, stunted, under-producing plants susceptible to drought, disease, and pests. The commonest and most fatal mistake of the first-time gardener is failure to thin ruthlessly enough.

You will want to save the strongest and fastest-growing plants. Pick the tardy and weak ones for thinning. If you are thinning outdoors, thin to the spacing suggested on the seed packet, or refer to each crop in the Fruits And Vegetables section of this book. If you are thinning indoor seedlings, thin to single plants in peat pots, or if you have planted in flats, thin enough to allow room to get each plant out for transplanting.

Transplanting Seedlings

If you've started seedlings indoors, moving them outside is going to be a shock to them. If you have a cold frame or a sheltered porch, you can prepare the plants by setting them out there for a week or ten days before transplanting. This is called "hardening off" the seedlings. Even an open window in the vicinity of your indoor-grown seedlings will assist the transition.

As you get seedlings used to harsher temperatures, cut back drastically on the amount of water you're giving them. This will not weaken the plants, but slow their rapid early growth so that they consolidate their strength for the trip outdoors.

When the time comes — an overcast, shady day is the best time — make suitable-sized holes in the outdoor garden for your seedlings. There should be enough room to accommodate all the earth that the seedlings' roots have occupied indoors — either all the soil in the individual pot, or all the soil around the roots if you have used a flat. Water the garden before you transplant, being careful not to re-fill the holes with earth. A good method is to fill the holes with water and wait for it to sink into the surrounding soil.

If you've grown many plants in one container, like a flat, you'll find that their roots have become entangled. Rather than try to pull them apart, section the box with a knife in much the same way as you would cut a cake into squares. The roots will recover from cutting much more readily than they will from tearing.

Try to handle all seedlings by the earth-ball, roots, or even leaves. But don't touch the delicate, vital stem if you can help it. It is easily damaged. When positioning seedlings in the ground, hold them by the leaves. New leaves can replace damaged ones, but a bruised young stem doesn't recover.

Bury your plants a little deeper than the 3 inches of soil they've been growing in. This is particularly helpful if you're burying the entire container, such as a peat pot. Get the top edge of the peat pot a good ¼ inch below the surface. Plants like tomatoes, which will grow roots all along their stems, can even be planted sideways, with the end of the stem turned up above the ground. They'll grow upwards from then on, and you will have a better root system developing underground.

After planting, fill the hole up with some of the soil you dug out before. Tamp it firmly around the plant with your fingers so the roots are nestled snugly in the soil.

When seedlings sprout, they should be thinned to proper distance. Outdoors, thin to spacing recommended for each crop on the seed packet, or in the Fruits And Vegetables section of this book. Indoors, thin pot-grown seedlings to one plant per pot, and flat-grown seedlings to one plant every 2 inches.

Use a scissors for cutting the weakest seedlings. Pulling them up will disturb the roots of the remaining seedlings. Be ruthless, because you are aiming for the health of the remaining plants.

The remaining plants will have room to grow to their full height and strength.

The easiest way to protect newly transplanted seedlings is to prop a board or other shield alongside the row to protect the plants from direct sun till they're settled in.

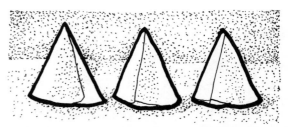

"Hot-Kaps," which are paper shields, and other protectors such as plastic bags, glass cups or jars, can be placed over the newly planted seedlings at night. They must be removed the next morning.

Weeding And Cultivating

You should keep all weeds out of your garden for the simple reason that they will compete with your vegetables for water, nutrients, and space to grow. It is best, of course, to catch the weeds at an early stage. All weeds should be removed before you set in any plants or seedlings. From then on a regular treatment with a flat hoe should keep the weeds from making a comeback. Weekends only is regular enough for any garden. "Work" the soil by using the hoe to pull out visible weeds and loosen the top inch of soil throughout the garden. The loosening process is called "cultivating" and is necessary for keeping the roots of plants aerated even when, in midsummer, few weeds are sprouting. Be careful not to disturb the young vegetable plants. If you find weeds growing in the midst of your vegetables, you'll have to pull them up by hand or snip them off at ground level.

Mulching

The easiest method of controlling weeds is mulching. Mulching is simply covering the ground around your plants with another substance, called mulch. Mulch can be organic, like straw, dead leaves, peat moss, or even torn-up newspapers. This covering will not only keep weeds from growing, but it will also keep moisture in the soil from evaporating quickly, keep soil from eroding in heavy rain, and keep the sun from "baking" the surface of the soil and damaging top roots. (If you use mulch, you may not need to loosen the soil so frequently either.) As the mulch decomposes it will even add nutrients to the soil.

If you use organic material for mulch, spread it in between rows and plants when the plants are about 6 inches high. The mulch should be about 2 inches deep after it gets wet and settles. Water and weed the garden before you mulch; then give the mulch a good soaking afterwards.

Some people use black polyethylene sheets as a mulch. This has all the advantages of organic mulch, except that it doesn't decompose into the soil. It's probably easier to put down than organic mulch, however. If you use black plastic, make sure to poke enough holes in it for water to

The flat hoe is used to scrape the surface of the soil near plant roots. Larger, deeply rooted weeds must be pulled by hand, or cut out with a cultivating hoe.

reach the soil beneath. Hold the sheeting down with rocks, sections of boards, or stakes poked through it at the corners.

Watering

The amount of watering you should do will be determined by the weather conditions in your area. You shouldn't set up a watering schedule to be followed blindly no matter how much sun or rain you get.

Watch your plants and soil. Do they look wilted or dry? How long has it been since the garden got any rain or watering? If it's been a week, it's probably time to water. On the other hand, a light sprinkle that fell for five minutes yesterday might have wet the surface, but not really reached the roots. You can always stick a finger down into the soil to see if it's damp beneath the surface.

When you do water, you should water thoroughly, so there is enough to reach deep roots. To penetrate 12 inches into the soil, you should have 3 inches of water.

Watering by sprinkling the entire garden is somewhat wasteful, but it will do the job. If you can, a better method is to flood the garden with water, channeling a small hose stream down each row in turn. Water slowly, so the water can seep into the soil. If it disappears quickly, you have not yet watered the soil enough. Hills of plants are perhaps best watered individually.

Trees close to your garden, especially willows, can send out roots that will interfere with plant growth. Prevent this by installing an underground "wall," 15 to 20 inches deep, between your garden and nearby trees. This barrier can be a sheet of metal, plastic or even tar paper.

People wonder how they can tell when they have provided 3 inches of water to a garden. Simple – just put out a pan where you are sprinkling. When there are 3 inches of water in the pan, there are 3 inches of water in the garden as well. The 3 inches will penetrate about 12 inches deep in the soil.

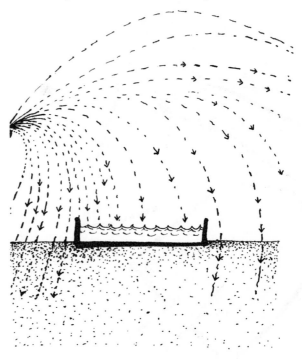

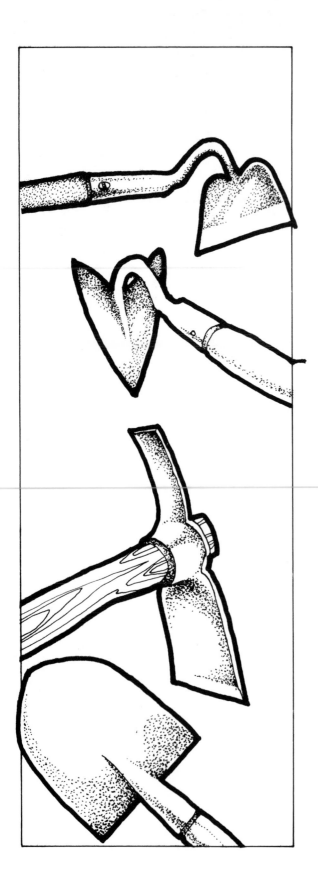

Garden Tools

Good tools are a wise investment for your garden. You can get cheap tools, you can make do with what you have around the house, you can borrow somebody else's tools. But your own good tools — and not very many at that — will last many seasons, will be there when you need them, and will save you a lot of extra labor in your garden.

Hoes

The tool you use most often will be a hoe. Hoes are used for planting, for cultivating, weeding, and preparing the ground in the fall and spring.

The ordinary flat-bladed hoe that everybody knows is used for shallow work: scraping the surface to remove small weeds and keep the topsoil from getting crusty. The drawback is that it isn't a precise tool, and may be clumsy to use between narrow rows and near the roots of plants.

The cultivating hoe has a triangular blade which offers considerable precision. It is particularly useful for cutting out larger, deeply rooted weeds between rows, and for careful scraping close in to your vegetable plants. However, it is harder to control the depth of its cut, so use this hoe carefully. Use a cultivating hoe for loosening the soil deeply before you plant root crops.

The grub hoe is a very heavy tool that has a flat hoe-shaped blade on one side, and sometimes a pickaxe-type pointed blade on the other side. It is used for hard work like rolling back turf, getting under rocks and roots to lift them out, and loosening hard, compacted soil. Some grub hoes have an axe-like blade instead of the pick; this is used for cutting through tree roots. If you live on rugged land, you will probably need a grub hoe.

Shovels And Forks

These are the tools for big jobs — for digging and for turning the soil. The shovel is a basic, necessary tool for digging the kinds of holes you need for transplanting plants that have been started elsewhere; for unearthing the "hills" that are the plant sites for many vegetables; and for moving earth from one place to another. The shovel is also used for turning over the dirt after fertilizing and prior to loosening up the clods in spring and fall.

Use the garden fork for the deep loosening you want to give the soil where your root crops grow. A fork is also used for turning a compost heap, and sometimes instead of a hoe for breaking clods and mixing in fertilizer.

Wheelbarrows

The old-time wheelbarrow with one wheel, a basket, and two arms is out-moded. By all means get yourself one of the modern, two-wheeled carts that don't tip.

Hand Tools

Some general words of advice: Hand tools are for hands. The most important thing is that they feel comfortable in *your* hands — and it is often the case that a good tool for a husband feels clumsy or heavy to a wife. Hold the tool before you buy it — is the handle comfortable? Does the weight feel balanced in your hand?

A hand pruner is necessary for shaping and caring for the dwarf fruit trees and grape vines suggested in this book. It is not, of course, necessary for vegetables. Be sure to get a pruner with a good steel blade, and test the spring action to make sure it is not going to be too hard on your hand muscles.

Scissors are useful for snipping twine ties in your garden, and a large pocket knife will come in handy at harvest time — particularly for squashes and cabbage heads. Again, good steel is worth the extra money.

A yardstick is useful at planting time. Use it to measure distances between rows to set the stakes in properly, and then lay the yardstick alongside the row as you plant to space seeds and plants correctly. The yardstick is useful when you thin the plants too.

Hand forks are good for lifting seedlings from a flat for transplanting, and for loosening weeds growing among your vegetable plants.

Hand spades come in narrow and wide shapes. The narrow one is most often used. Dig your transplanting holes with a hand spade, and, if you like, scrape shallow drills with its point for planting small seeds. The wider hand spade is convenient for putting soil into pots and flats, fertilizer into hills, or for digging the

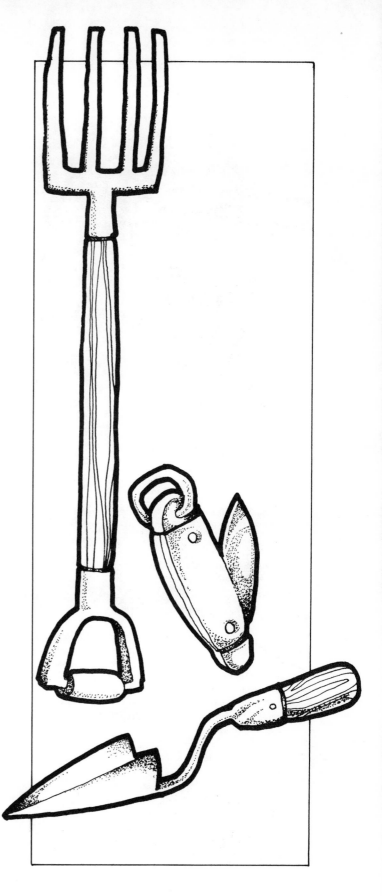

There are three types of garden sprayers. The hose-end jar sprayer is the least expensive, but the hose may impede your movement around the garden. The hand-operated compression type sprayer costs more. It can be tiring and inefficient to use for very large jobs, but is fine for most gardeners. A battery-operated power sprayer is the easiest to use for large jobs like spraying fruit trees if you are willing to make the investment.

Dusters are cardboard tubes usually sold containing insecticide or fungicide in powder form. The tube slides open and closed, like a trombone, expelling dust.

Remember that the finer the cloud of spray or dust, the better. Keep the spray nozzle or duster moving back and forth as you work. Spray from underneath, aiming upward at an angle to cover both sides of the leaves.

larger holes you will need for transplanting nursery-grown tomato plants.

Inexperienced hands may avoid blisters by using garden gloves. Leather ones last longer, but they are quite hot. Canvas ones "breathe," but must be replaced more often.

Coping With Pests And Diseases

A variety of troubles can befall your garden plants. Insects, birds and small animals may show up to feast at the table you have prepared for them. Diseases, brought on in part by bad weather, bad soil, or bad luck, can ruin a lot of work and hope. All these can be prevented or fought off, however; and then again, they may not happen at all.

Your basic defense is to grow strong plants. Space the plants widely enough apart so they have growing room. Cultivate your soil. Dig out the weeds. Check nursery-grown plants for signs of insects or disease before you buy them.

Each fall, clear your garden of all vegetation, so insects and blights don't have a chance to winter over. Pull the old plants up and throw them on your compost pile, where the heat of decomposition will kill blights. Turn over the ground with a shovel.

If you rotate your crops as much as possible — planting them in different places from year to year, you can help prevent disease.

Diseases

If trouble does develop, be alert for it. If only one plant is affected, get rid of the plant right away. The most common problem is "damping off," which occurs when seedlings are just sprouting or have been transplanted outdoors from a house or cold frame. You can come out one morning to find one or all of your seedlings tipped over at ground level as if bitten off. Close examination will show that a part of the stem at or near ground level is intact, but mushy and rotten. This is damping off, caused by a fungus and aggravated by moving the plants outside too early. One prevention is to plant seedlings indoors only in sterilized soil or pots. Commercial potting soil and planting mediums such as peat pots or peat pellets are safely sterilized. The only cure is to start over again with new seedlings.

Other fungi can attack your plants in a variety of ways, often producing an easily recognizable misshapen plant, root, fruit, or leaf. "Dead spots" on leaves, powdery deposits, and yellowing leaves can also be signs of diseases. If in doubt, bring a leaf or branch into your garden dealer for his opinion and advice. He will be able to supply the proper fungicides. Be careful to follow the directions on the label. More is definitely not better, in the case of fungicides and insecticides.

Insect Pests

The first time you see an insect on your tenderly nurtured plants, remember: Not all insects eat plants. Some eat other insects, and they are your friends. So don't take drastic measures until you see actual damage.

If you find your plants cut off at the bottom when they are young (check to see it's not damping off) you may be a victim of cutworms. A preventive measure is the use of collars.

If the leaves of your plants seem to be covered with a sticky, colorless substance, you have aphids. Remove the affected leaf and any other fresh leaves showing stickiness or signs of wilt. Aphids are tiny, pale-colored but sometimes brown or black insects, no more than ⅛ inch long. They're hard to see, but once you know they're there you can knock them off the plant with a strong spray of water.

Spider mites are another tiny nuisance. You can usually tell they're around by the speckled yellow look that leaves take on when spider mites are eating them. Water spray helps here too. Repeat often.

The cabbage worm, or looper (because of the way it loops itself up to crawl) will attack all members of the cabbage family. Pick these and all pale green, many–legged worms off the plants and kill them. Such worms can attack cucumbers, squash and tomatoes, among other plants.

Ladybugs are helpful insects, but similar beetles with a yellow or white color and various spots or stripes may attack vegetable foliage.

What about insecticides? Most informed people are aware of the danger of pollution that insecticides may cause. We have read about or tried organic substitutes like soapsud sprays, and mixtures made with water and garlic, onions, marigold leaves, hot peppers, and tomato

To prevent cabbage cutworms a stiff cardboard, plastic or tar-paper collar is slipped over the plant and pushed at least an inch into the ground with 2 inches or more above ground. The collar shouldn't be tight – leave at least ½-inch clearance on all sides for the plant to grow.

Helpful insects include ladybugs, praying mantises, and wasps – three that just about anyone can recognize. The common pink earthworm (though not an insect) is helpful too, because it burrows underground, aerating and cultivating the soil for easy root growth. Look in organic garden magazines for ladybugs, mantises and earthworms that you can buy for your garden.

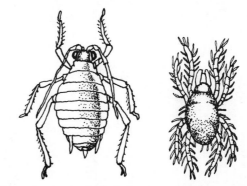

Damaging insects include the tiny aphid and spider-mite (shown here magnified), the cutworm, "loopers" or "inchworms," and the cucumber and squash beetles.

Chain link fence, 3 feet high, runs about $1.20 a foot. Price includes toprails and posts. The gate is another $30.00.

Picket fencing comes 4 feet high in 50 foot rolls for about $35.00 a roll. Posts vary according to the kind you buy. Picket gates are as low as $10.00.

Stockade fencing is sold in sections 4 feet high and 8 feet long for $20.00 or more per section. Posts, one every 8 feet, are about $3.50 each. Matching gates are $22.00.

leaves. Some work in some situations. We encourage you to try your luck with them.

Derris (rotenone) and pyrethrum-based sprays and dusts are advertised as safe to humans. If you feel that spraying with chemicals is a necessity, you can use them. It's wise to remember that DDT used to be considered safe too, so wash your fruits and vegetables well before eating them.

Animal Pests

Birds of all kinds will eat your seeds from the ground and the fruit of some vegetables later on. Fending off birds can be an intriguing project for the whole family. Scarecrows become useless when birds get used to them, and a different "scare" has to replace the old. Strings with tin foil, pop-tops from cans, or jingle bells strung over the garden sometimes work.

Animals such as rabbits, woodchucks and raccoons will find your plants appetizing. Deer are a problem in some areas. Fences will discourage animals, but raccoons can climb and a few determined rabbits and woodchucks may burrow under. Deer can leap fences, but are not likely to. Dogs can keep animals away, but then you have to persuade your dog not to dig or romp in the garden.

Fences

Besides discouraging wild animals, you may want to fence in your garden so that you and your neighbors' dogs, cats, and children can stay on good terms.

Chain link fence is probably the most effective, though perhaps not the most attractive. It is not the easiest fence to install; its weight calls for posts sunk in concrete, and assembly requires wrench and pliers to bolt sections together.

A picket fence can be purchased preassembled in rolls. Put a few posts in the ground and you can unroll the picket around your garden.

If you're really troubled by small animals invading your garden, you can put up stockade fencing, which is like picket fencing with no spaces in between the pickets.

Less expensive (and less decorative) is the galvanized fence roll. This is easy to put up, needing only a few posts, and is inexpensive.

A steel mesh fence with a vinyl coating (for durability and for extra safety from sharp edges) is just as easy to install and about the same price.

Split-rail fences are very popular, but they keep very little out. If you want a split rail fence, especially if you are going to espalier dwarf fruit trees or train grape vines along it, you can always tack a roll of chicken wire to it to keep out animals. The chicken wire is almost invisible from a distance. Chicken wire fencing, sold as rolls, is the cheapest of all fences.

Installing Fence Posts

The big job in installing any fence is sinking the fence posts in the ground. Chain link, split rail, and other fences that you buy in kits or from a dealer will come supplied with posts. Fencing that you buy in roll form may not. Check with your dealer for the best advice on what size and type of post to buy.

Steel posts, because they are narrow and only used to support light fencing, can usually be installed just by hammering into the ground.

Wooden posts should be at least 2 inches by 4 inches, preferably 4 inches by 4 inches. Unless the posts are rot-resistant like redwood, cypress, or cedar, they should be painted with creosote up to the soil line before you set them into their holes. One way to be sure the post stays firmly in its hole is to nail a cleat to the bottom of the post. A cleat is simply a piece of 2 by 4 that is 6 to 8 inches long. It is nailed into the bottom of the post to make a T-shaped base. Dig a hole in the ground wide enough to accommodate the cleat, a little more than a foot deep. Fill the hole with soil and tamp the ground down tightly.

A second method is to dig a 12-inch deep hole, 3 times the diameter of the post you're installing. Fill the hole with wet concrete after setting the post in it. Let the concrete harden around the post, propping the post up straight if necessary during the drying period.

If your fence is not a heavy one, you can simply use a post digger (rent from a garden store) or a narrow shovel for digging a narrow hole in the ground, about 18 inches deep. Set the post into the hole, and fill with either concrete or tamped-down soil.

Split rail fencing comes in separate parts – posts, rails, and end posts. It works out to about $14 for each 10-foot section, with another $26.00 for a split rail gate.

Galvanized fence comes in rolls 3 feet high and 50 feet long for about $17.00 a roll. Posts can be steel, one every 6 feet, at $2.80 each.

Chicken wire comes in rolls 3 feet high and 50 feet long from $7.00 to $10.00, depending on the thickness of the wire. The inexpensive steel posts are sufficient to support it.

2
The Fruits And Vegetables

Tomatoes

The tomato is one vegetable you'll be glad to grow. It's easy to take care of — even with no care, you'll get some fruit. And if you've never tasted tomatoes that have ripened on the vine to a rich, red maturity, you're in for a treat. Store-bought tomatoes are picked green and ripen in shipping. But they reach ripeness without really maturing.

There are many kinds of tomatoes, from tiny ½-inch fruit that you can grow in a flower pot to huge beefsteak tomatoes that can weigh a couple of pounds each. Plant several different kinds to see what you like best. Include a few early-flowering plants.

Tomato Varieties

The best flavored cocktail-sized tomato is Small Fry. Good early varieties with full-size fruit are Early Girl and Starfire. Ultra Girl VFN is an early variety that is very resistant to disease. Early Fireball is good if you live in the extreme northern part of the United States. All of these varieties will have green tomatoes within two months after being planted outdoors as seedlings.

Good mid-summer tomatoes for the best eating are numerous. Burpee's Big Boy, Ultra Boy VFN and Wonder Boy VF Hybrid are good types. Seed catalogs are your best guide to the new varieties constantly being developed.

If you're going to use tomatoes for making tomato paste or sauces, grow Roma, Red Top, or San Marzano varieties, which give very meaty flesh. Good varieties for canning because of their intense color, resistance to cracks and few seeds are Moira, Heinz 1350, and Campbell 19.

Tomato Cultivation

Tomatoes are easiest to grow from well-developed potted plants available at garden stores. If you'd rather start tomatoes indoors from seed, get started 6 to 8 weeks before you expect to be able to transplant to the garden. Transplanting is less risky if you use individual 4-inch pots instead of flats. Tomatoes are very sensitive to frost, so don't move them outside until the last frost has come and gone. Plant seeds ½ inch deep. If you're planting them directly outside, plant in drills, or rows, one seed every 3 to 6 inches in a furrow you've made with your finger.

Inside or out, the seedling tomato plants should be thinned after they're 2 inches tall. If you're staking the plants — and we think you should, to prevent damage from the fruit lying on the ground — a distance of 18 inches between plants is enough. If you don't stake, leave 3 feet of space between plants and rows because branches will spread along the ground.

Tomatoes need a lot of water. You will find that they like watering more often than once a week. And if you neglect them, they'll let you know right away by drooping and curling their leaves. Fortunately, they'll snap right back after a good watering. The only trouble will be that if the plant has developed fruit already, they'll be more likely to ripen with cracks in them. The drying out causes the fruit to contract and replenishment with water causes them to expand, splitting the skin. The use of a mulch, particularly the black plastic kind, can lessen the need to water frequently.

Pick tomatoes when they've turned red and have had a few extra days on the vine to reach full juiciness. In the fall, pick your green tomatoes before the first frost comes to prevent damage. Ripen them inside on a windowsill, or slow down the ripening by keeping the fruit in a dark place like a closet or basement.

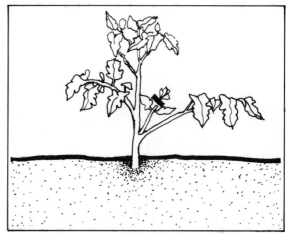

Tomato plants are prone to develop "suckers", which are branches that grow from the axil between a side branch and the main stem. To encourage strong growth and large fruit, it is best to pinch suckers off as they appear.

A good way to stake tomatoes is to build a teepee of sticks to support 3 plants; bind the teepee top with string, then tie the plants to each "leg" as they grow.

Tomatoes in any variety can be expected to yield heavily. Largest crops are from vine-type plants, but they grow to 5 or 6 feet and require substantial staking if you want to protect the fruit from damage from lying on the ground. If you don't wish to stake, pick tomatoes daily as the crop begins to ripen. The 2 to 3-foot bush-types are more usual in home gardens.

To peel tomatoes, plunge them into boiling water for 1 minute or less. Rinse immediately in cold water. The skin will now come off easily in large thin peels.

Note: Detailed information for preserving foods safely by boiling water-bath, hot water-bath and steam-pressure methods will be found on pages 74 and 75.

Tomato Recipes

Green Tomato Relish

4 quarts cored chopped green tomatoes (about 32 medium)	2 tablespoons mustard seed
1 large head chopped cabbage	1 tablespoon celery seed
4 medium sweet red peppers, chopped	½ cup salt
	1 ½ cups brown sugar
4 ½ cups cider vinegar	1 tablespoon whole cloves
3 large onions chopped	2 whole allspice
	1 tablespoon prepared horseradish

Sprinkle the salt over all the vegetables and let stand for 4 hours. Press in a colander and drain to remove free liquid. Add the sugar, horseradish, and spice to the vinegar and simmer for 15 minutes. Then add vegetables and heat to boiling. Pack immediately into hot jars, leaving a space of ⅛ inch at top of jar. Process in boiling water-bath for 10 minutes. Yield: about 7 pints.

Tomato Catsup

4 quarts tomatoes (about 24 large)	1 teaspoon whole allspice
4 medium onions, chopped	4 bay leaves
	1 cinnamon stick
1 medium sweet red pepper, chopped	1½ cups cider vinegar
1 teaspoon mustard seed	1 tablespoon paprika
	1 tablespoon salt
	1 cup vinegar

Peel, core, and chop tomatoes and combine with the onions and pepper. Cook until soft. Remove from the stove and put ingredients through a food mill. Return to stove and boil until the volume is decreased by about half, stirring frequently. This should take about an hour. Combine the whole spices and put into a cheesecloth bag or large tea ball. Add this with the sugar and salt to the tomato mixture and cook for another 25 minutes, still stirring frequently. Add the vinegar and paprika and cook, stirring, until thick. When the catsup reaches the desired consistency, pour immediately into hot canning jars, leaving ⅛-inch space at top. Cover and process in boiling water-bath for 10 minutes. Yield: about 3 pints.

Stewed Tomatoes

6 large ripe tomatoes	herbs: basil, oregano
1 green pepper, diced	or tarragon
1 large onion, diced	4 tablespoons butter
1 tablespoon fresh	salt and pepper to taste

Peel the tomatoes, leave them whole or cut in halves or quarters. Put into saucepan with diced onion, green pepper, fresh herbs, and butter. Cover and simmer on low heat 10 minutes, or until the tomatoes soften somewhat and produce their own juice. Taste and season with salt and pepper. Pack whole into jars and either freeze, or process in boiling water-bath for 10 minutes before storing.

Tomato Sauces

Spaghetti sauces are a delicious and economic way to use your extra tomatoes. You can use any kind of tomato, but the Roma variety is best for its pungent taste. After you have made and preserved the basic tomato sauce, you can use it as a base for many famous sauces, each flavored with its own unique ingredients. Try to use fresh herbs wherever possible for the finest taste. If you can't, use dried herbs in half the amounts called for in the recipe. Experiment a bit with herbs. Everyone's palate is different, so use them to your own taste.

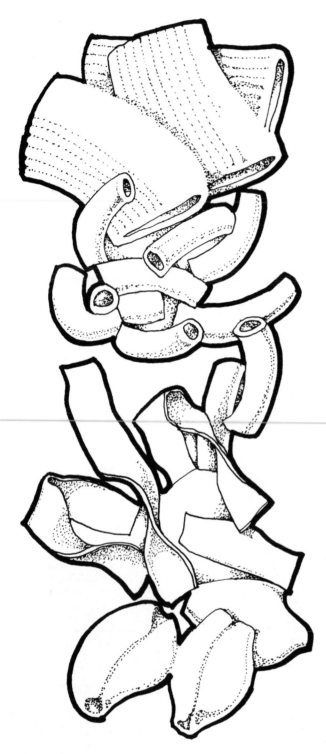

6 large fresh tomatoes, peeled and cored; or	2 tablespoons chopped fresh basil
4 cups canned tomatoes	
2 cloves garlic, pressed or minced	2 tablespoons chopped fresh parsley
½ teaspoon sugar	
1 bay leaf	1 tablespoon oregano leaves
1 large or 2 medium onions, chopped or sliced	
3 tablespoons olive oil	salt and pepper to taste

Heat the olive oil over a low flame. Add the chopped onions and garlic and cook for about 3 minutes, or until translucent, stirring often. Add the tomatoes and the rest of the ingredients. Cook the sauce uncovered at a low heat until it thickens (45 minutes or longer). Stir occasionally so it will not burn or stick. Remove from the stove and put through a food mill to puree, or don't bother if a rougher texture suits you. Add more seasoning if desired. Yield: about 1 quart.

If you want to make the sauce in large quantities, you can freeze or can it. Can by processing in the boiling water bath for 30 minutes.

Each of the following variations can be made from scratch, using the basic tomato sauce procedure and adding the unique ingredients that give the sauce its special flavor. Or, simply use the basic sauce from your freezer or cans, and add the special ingredients.

Marinara Sauce: Saute 8 finely chopped anchovies in their own oil until they are mushy. Add 1 quart of tomato sauce and stir in the chopped parsley. Heat and serve.

If you are starting from scratch, you would saute the anchovies right along with the onion and garlic, and add the parsley just before you serve the sauce.

Meat Sauce: Brown 1 pound ground beef and ¼ pound ground pork or sausage in a heavy pot. Stir and crush the meat until there are no lumps, and all the meat is cooked. Add 1 quart of basic sauce and heat to boiling. Add ½ pound sliced mushrooms and 1 tablespoon chopped parsley and cook another 15 minutes before serving.

If you are starting from scratch, add the meat to the onion and garlic mixture as soon as it is done, and brown the meat with the onions before adding tomatoes. Add mushrooms and parsley 15 minutes before serving.

Zucchini Beef Sauce: Brown 1 pound ground beef in a heavy pot. Stir and crush the meat until there are no lumps and all the meat is cooked. Add 2 medium zucchini, sliced, and 2 medium green peppers, chopped. Cook over medium heat, stirring frequently, until mixture loses enough water to hold its shape on a spoon. Add 1 quart basic sauce, 1 tablespoon parsley, and heat to boiling.

To start from scratch, add meat to onion and garlic mixture as soon as it is cooked, and brown together. Zucchini and peppers can be added with the tomatoes, but the sauce will require a somewhat longer time to boil down to a thick sauce. Tomato paste is often helpful for thickening watery sauces.

If you wish to make very large quantities of tomato sauce for freezing or canning, these are the ingredients for 4 gallons of sauce:

2 dozen large fresh tomatoes or 16 cups canned tomatoes
8 cloves garlic
2 teaspoons sugar
4 bay leaves
4 Bermuda onions
12 tablespoons olive oil
8 tablespoons fresh basil (or 4 tablespoons dried basil)
8 tablespoons fresh parsley (or 4 tablespoons dried parsley)
4 tablespoons oregano
2 tablespoons salt
1 tablespoon pepper

You will have to cook the sauce longer to get it to thicken – about 2 hours.

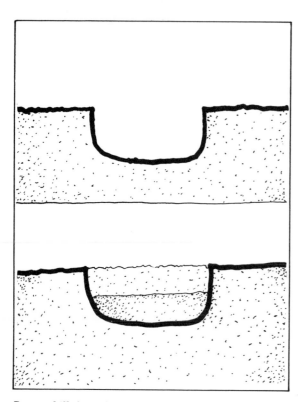

Prepare hills by making a hole in the ground about 8 inches deep and 1 foot across. Fill the bottom 4 inches of the hole with dried manure. Cover the earth to ground level. Plant about 9 seeds ½ inch deep at equal distances around the edge of the hole. When the seedlings are 6 to 8 inches tall, thin to 3 plants per hill. One hill will give you about 70 cucumbers. For more than one hill, space 5 feet apart.

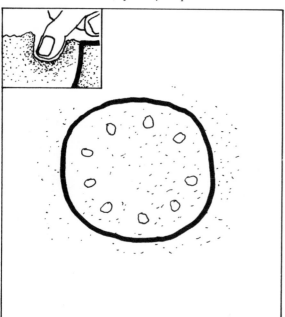

Cucumbers

There are three kinds of cucumbers. The European or seedless type can only be grown in greenhouses. They are very demanding in their feeding requirements, too.

The other two kinds are the slicing kind and the pickling kind. The slicing kind tend to grow bigger and have a sweeter taste than the pickling kind, but there's no hard and fast division between them. Since cucumbers can be harvested at any time after the fruit has set, you can pick very small ones of any kind for pickling. And if you want to go ahead and eat the pickling kind raw or in a salad, that's fine if you like the taste.

Some people find raw cucumbers hard to digest. Recently, varieties have been developed which are "bitter free," or "burpless," so you might try some of these if you haven't liked cucumbers in the past.

Cucumber Varieties

The best of the new "burpless" varieties is Sweet Slice, although more new varieties are being developed. Some other slicing varieties are Straight 8, Marketer, Marketmore 70, Burpee Hybrid, Tablegreen, and Palmetto. Pickling varieties include National Pickling, Double Yield Pickling, and Wisconsin S.M.R. 12.

Some varieties that we have not recommended are "gynoecious hybrids." This means the fruiting plants are all female; they produce unusually heavy yields. These must be planted with a few male plants. (One male plant will service many female plants.) If you buy a seed packet of an unfamiliar variety, and find that a few of the seeds are colored green (the male seeds) they are gynoecious hybrid seeds. We don't advise use of these hybrids for a small home garden. They're primarily for farmers who want as large a yield as possible and have enough plants to make this kind of growing possible.

Cucumber Cultivation

You can start cucumbers indoors in small pots or flats, but because their growing season is short, it's not necessary. If you plant seeds directly into the ground outdoors, you will be harvesting in about two months. However, the seeds will not germinate in cold ground — below 60° — so if you're impatient, it's possible to start the plants indoors. Just remember to plant them only about two to four weeks before you can move them outside, or you'll have plants too big for small pots or flats, and their growth will be permanently stunted. Cucumbers are usually planted in hills.

Cucumbers need a lot of watering. Weeds growing nearby are especially harmful to cucumbers because they use up moisture in the ground. If you don't mulch, be sure and use a hoe to scrape the weeds out of the ground as soon as they appear. Follow the same general watering instructions as for tomatoes.

Don't let cucumbers ripen completely on the vine. If you do, the plant will stop producing. Pick while they're still green, before they turn yellow. They're ready to eat from the time they appear on the plant. Snip the stems with a scissors to avoid twisting the delicate vines.

Cucumber Pests

Watch out for cucumber beetles, which have either 3 black stripes or 12 black spots on the wings, depending on the variety. The pickleworm also is a cucumber lover. This is a yellowish worm about ¾ inch long, with a brown head. Pick pickleworms and cucumber beetles off your plants early in the morning, when you can still find them on top of the leaves. Pick off yellow or orange egg clusters on the underside of the leaves. Some people cover the entire hill of plants with cheesecloth early in the season to protect the plants until they get established.

To protect cucumbers from possible damage from lying on the ground, support the three vines on the hill with a cylinder of wire built to the outside of the plants while they are still young. The branches will grow over the support and droop like ivy, making harvesting the fruit easier too. Another way to support cucumbers is the tent of three sticks described on page 35; you can even train cucumbers along a wire fence.

Cucumbers can be harvested at different sizes depending on what you intend to do with them. Very young cucumbers are often used in sweet pickles, older ones for dills. However, if the cucumbers begin to turn yellow, you have left them on the vine too long. They will be seedy, not really crisp, and may be bitter as well.

Note: Detailed information for preserving foods safely by boiling water-bath, hot water-bath and steam-pressure methods will be found on pages 74 and 75.

This old-fashioned pottery crock is still the easiest container for curing dill pickles. It is wide enough to pack well, and an ordinary plate will fit to hold the pickles down under the brine. Level and straight sides make skimming the scum easier too. Such crocks are still to be found at reasonable prices at antique and second hand stores. If you can't get a lid, cover the crock with a clean cloth.

When you skim each day, be sure to wash the plate and weight, and to wipe the inside of the crock above the brine.

Pickle Recipes

Dill Pickles

The classic garlic and dill flavored whole pickle requires a two to four week curing period before the pickles are packed. There are quicker ways to make dill pickles, but no other method gives the same sharp flavor and texture as the old-fashioned way.

30 to 40 pickling cucumbers (about 5 inches long)	or dill seed
	4 cloves crushed garlic
3 tablespoons mixed pickling spices	1 ½ cups non-iodized salt
a dozen sprigs of dill (blossoms or leaves) or dry dill	5 peppercorns
	2 cups vinegar
	8 cups hot water

All utensils used for pickling should be made from enamelware, glass, or stainless steel. Other metal utensils may react with the salts or acid to cause undesirable color changes.

Select only slightly underripe, perfect cucumbers and try to start pickling while they are nice and fresh. Wash and dry the cucumbers thoroughly. Place a layer of dill, and half the spices and garlic in a clean crockery jar or stainless steel container. Place cucumbers on top and cover with remaining spices and dill.

Dissolve the salt in 4 to 6% acid vinegar and the water. Pour this mixture over the pickles and cover with a glass or china plate. Use a weight (a water-filled jar or a clean rock) to hold the plate down in the brine. Store in a cool place (60°-70°) for two to four weeks. Make certain that the cucumbers are covered with brine at all times so they don't discolor or spoil. If the brine gets low, make more brine solution and add to pickles. Each day remove any scum that has accumulated — scum can cause softening, discoloration and spoiling. To check "doneness," remove a pickle from the brine from time to time and slice. If there are no white areas and the pickles look translucent all the way through, they are ready.

Now pack the pickles into hot canning jars, leaving a little more than a ¼-inch space at top of jar. Strain the brine in which the cucumbers were cured and boil for 5 minutes. Pour this solution over pickles, leaving ¼-inch space at top of jar. Cover and process for 10 minutes. Yield: about 5 quarts.

Sweet Pickles

1 quart vinegar
2 cups water
1 ½ teaspoons
  pickling salt
1 tablespoon dill seeds

3 tablespoons
  non-iodized salt
8 to 10 pickling
  cucumbers

Soak pickles overnight in the water, vinegar, and salts. Add more liquid if pickles are not completely covered. Set a plate on top as for dills. Next day, drain the liquid and boil it. When it boils, add cucumbers again and turn off heat. Put the dill seeds into a clean jar and add the cucumbers. Reboil the liquid and fill jars to within ¼ inch of top. Make sure no air bubbles remain in jars by running a knife down the insides. You can add other ingredients to the jar at bottom or top, such as bay leaf, red pepper, garlic clove, fresh dill. Seal jar and process for 15 minutes.

Country-style Pickles

  Country style pickles can be made with many different ingredients. Try different combinations from your garden.

8 to 10 pickling size
  cucumbers (or
  equivalent bulk of
  mixed vegetables)

1 cup salt
4 quarts water
2 cups sugar
1 ½ cups vinegar

Wash and slice cucumbers into ½ inch slices. Slice and cube other ingredients into ½ inch cubes or slices. In cold water, dissolve the salt and let the vegetables soak in the brine for 12 to 16 hours in a cool (60°-70°) place. Drain. Add spices and sugar to vinegar and boil 3 minutes. Add the vegetables and simmer till thoroughly heated. Pack immediately into canning jar, leaving ⅛-inch headspace. Cover and process 15 minutes.

Some vegetables used in pickling are green tomatoes cut into thin slices, cauliflower broken into florets, tiny peeled onions or larger ones sliced, sweet red peppers with seeds and membranes removed, and string beans chopped to size.

Mustard pickles are prepared the same as country-style pickles up to the end of the 16 hour brine soaking period. Then mix 1½ cups sugar, 1 tablespoon tumeric, and ½ cup of flour, gradually adding ½ cup of water until smooth. Mix in ½ cup prepared mustard and 5 cups vinegar. Cook, stirring until mixture thickens. Add vegetables and simmer for 15 minutes. Then pack and process for 15 minutes.

Cabbage And Its Relatives

Cabbage Varieties

There are many varieties of cabbage, which mature at different times. All have a long growing season, from 110 to 170 days. Farmers grow them in sequences, providing for a season-long harvest. You will notice seed marked "early" and "late" variety. The days marked on the pack refer to the number of days to maturity from the time the seedlings are transplanted into the garden. In all but the southern United States, the early varieties must be started indoors, transplanted outside, and harvested before the really hot weather begins. Late varieties are planted later, can be started outdoors, and are harvested in the fall. You can simplify matters by planting both varieties at once and harvesting whenever they mature.

A third, "late storage" type of cabbage can be stored all winter, and is the best kind for sauerkraut or cole slaw. The storage coagulates the juices in the leaves so that when they are shredded, they hold their juice and crunchiness.

A good tasting early variety is Emerald Acre. Stokes Viking Golden Acre is an early variety that is disease resistant and will thrive in soil that is not heavily fertilized (unlike most cabbage). Stonehead is a "middle-early" variety that is disease resistant.

Two good varieties for late harvest are Greenback and Autumn Marvel.

Late varieties of cabbage form much larger heads than early varieties, but the total yield per row is about the same, since the larger late plants are spaced further apart.

When transplanting, plant seedlings deeper outside than they were in their indoor containers. This will help the stem to support the large head that will develop. Water immediately after transplanting, and tuck the soil in firmly to cover the roots. As the plant continues to grow, support the head with additional soil tucked underneath.

Late storage varieties that keep their green color and store for six months or more include Storage Green, April Green and Green Winter.

Red cabbage varieties include Meteor, Red Acre (disease resistant) and Red Head. Storage Red is good for winter storage.

Cabbage Cultivation

The time to plant cabbage depends a great deal on what variety you are growing and what the growing conditions will be like in your part of the country. Start early varieties indoors in February and March in very cold areas. Plant seeds ¼ inch deep, and thin to 2 inches apart. You may want to move seedlings to individual 4-inch pots when they grow larger. Set plants outside in rows 2 or 3 feet apart, with the plants 14 inches apart. Do this five or six weeks after starting seedlings, even if you still have frost in your area.

For late cabbage in most parts of the country, the simplest procedure is to start the seeds indoors along with the early varieties and plant them together. If you have winters where the temperature doesn't go below 30°, you will have too warm a summer for growing late cabbages, but you can plant them in late September and harvest in March. Late varieties grow larger, and should be transplanted 20 inches apart in rows that are 36 inches apart.

Cabbage must have abundant water during its growing season. If it dries out and then is watered heavily, heads can crack or burst.

Cabbage roots grow close to the surface, so be careful when using your hoe to dig up weeds. A mulch may be the best solution.

Fertilizing the cabbage row during the growing season is a good idea, since cabbages are heavy feeders. About a month after transplanting, scatter by hand some dried manure or dried blood meal between the plants — enough to lightly cover the ground.

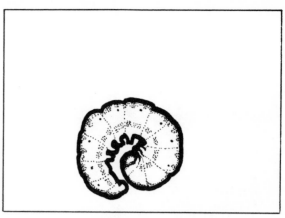

Mature cabbages may be attacked by cabbage worms. Look for velvety, inch-long worms the same color as the cabbage leaf and kill them. They lay egg clusters on the bottoms of the leaves, which should also be removed and destroyed.

Newly-transplanted cabbages suffer from cutworm and from damping off. See page 31 for how to avoid cutworm destruction. The best solution to early damage by damping off is to keep a supply of seedlings growing in pots or a cold frame to replace ruined plants until they are established.

Newer cabbage varieties are resistant to disease, but make sure anyway that if you plant cabbage next year it is in a different part of the garden. This rotation helps prevent cabbage diseases from thriving in the soil.

You'll know when it's time to harvest cabbage by the solid firmness of the head. Pull it out of the ground, root and all. Cut off the root with a sharp knife and remove the outer leaves of the head.

If left in the ground past harvest time, cabbage heads will split open. No problem — make sauerkraut from the split heads. But cracking of one can be a signal that the others are ready to harvest.

Late cabbage heads kept for storage should be in good condition — solid and tight. They will keep for several months in a cold frame where the temperature is in the 30's or below. The root cellar described on page 55 is useful for storing cabbage heads too.

Cauliflower And Brussels Sprouts

These two vegetables are grown in much the same way as their cousins the cabbages. Once the cauliflower plants develop heads about teacup size, they must be blanched. Do this on a dry day by drawing the outside leaves together to cover the inner head, and tying them. Grow them this way till it's time to harvest. The Snowball varieties are the ones to plant. Cauliflower is more sensitive to cold than cabbage and shouldn't be transplanted until after the last frost. The sprouts of brussels sprouts ripen from the bottom up — the lowest sprouts ripen about four months after the seed was planted. The rest continue to ripen, from bottom to top, over a six week period. To speed harvest on plants that have been transplanted outside after the last frost in spring, pinch off the top of the brussels sprouts stalk. Frost won't hurt these plants until well into winter. Those sprouts that mature after a fall frost have the best flavor. Jade Cross hybrid is the most popular variety.

Unlike most vegetables which are grown for their leaves, roots, or fruits, cauliflower and broccoli are grown for their immature blossom heads. There is little difference between the two plants botanically, but cauliflower is blanched, while broccoli is left alone to stay green. Otherwise, cultivation is the same. Harvest broccoli while the flower head is still tight and deep green.

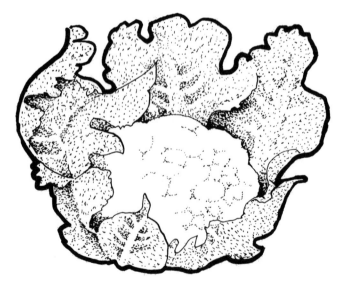

Cabbage Recipes

Cabbage Relish

4 cups finely chopped cabbage
4 cups chopped onion
6 chopped hot red peppers
12 chopped green peppers
4 cups chopped green tomatoes
2 cups chopped carrots or chopped celery
½ cup salt
4 cups sugar
4 cups cider vinegar
2 cups water
2 teaspoons mustard seed

Combine cabbage, onions, tomatoes, peppers, carrots, and salt. Let stand overnight. Then mix remaining ingredients in a saucepan and bring to a boil. Simmer for 4 minutes. Add rinsed and drained vegetables and cook 10 minutes. Pour into sterilized jars and process in boiling water-bath for 10 minutes. Yield: 4 quarts.

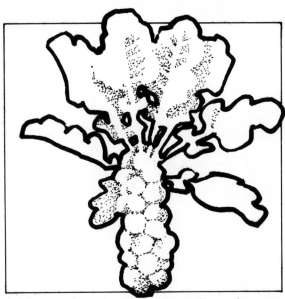

It is fun to try brussels sprouts just to see the way the sprouts grow. Maturing of the sprouts is hastened by cutting off the top of the plant to stop stalk growth in early September.

Cole Slaw

Cole slaw is finely-shredded cabbage moistened with a sauce. One of the easiest sauces is made of equal parts mayonnaise and heavy cream. Add vinegar, salt, and sugar to taste. For extra flavor, add chopped parsley, chives or other herbs, or dry hot mustard.

German Red Cabbage

1 head of red cabbage
4 slices chopped bacon or salt pork
4 tablespoons chopped onions
2 apples cored, peeled and thinly sliced
⅛ teaspoon caraway seed
¼ teaspoon salt
¼ cup vinegar or ½ cup red wine

Remove the outer leaves from the cabbage and cut into quarters. Cut out the core, and shred the cabbage quarters. Over a low heat cook the bacon until some of the fat is rendered. Add onion to bacon and sauté till golden. Put the cabbage in a pot, add apples, caraway seeds, sautéd onion, salt and vinegar or wine. Cover and simmer slowly for 1 hour and 20 minutes, adding a little water if necessary.

Note: Detailed information for preserving foods safely by boiling water-bath, hot water-bath and steam-pressure methods will be found on pages 74 and 75.

Sauerkraut

Sauerkraut is made by allowing cabbage to ferment in salt brine. For a good texture, use firm, ripe cabbage. Old, woody cabbages make mushy sauerkraut. The salt should be non-iodized kosher or pickling salt, since iodized salt will darken the cabbage. The salt and cabbage are combined in the proportion of 3 tablespoons of salt to 5 pounds of shredded cabbage. If you want to experiment a bit you can add caraway, dill, bay leaves, or garlic to the mix. Use whole peeled cloves of garlic so they can be fished out before serving.

Preparing the Cabbage: Trim off the outer leaves and wash the cabbage heads. Cut into quarters and remove the cores. Shred with a sharp knife or use a shredder if you have one. Mix the shredded cabbage together with the salt in a large container and let it stand for 3 to 5 minutes. It will wilt slightly and be easier to pack without breaking or bruising. Some people alternate layers of salt and cabbage while they pack, instead of mixing them beforehand.

Packing the Cabbage: Use a clean crock or large glass jar. You may be able to find old crocks in second-hand stores. Storage is better if you can find crocks with lids. Allow 5 pounds of prepared cabbage for each gallon of the container.

Place part of the cabbage and salt mixture in the bottom of the crock. Press down firmly on the mixture with a wooden spoon or a jar bottom. This will start the juice flowing. Continue adding shredded cabbage, salt (and seasonings if you are using any), tamping down each layer until the jar or crock is full.

Cover the cabbage with a sterile cloth (one that has been boiled for 10 minutes), and put a weight on it. If you are using a large crock, cover the cloth with a clean plate, held down with a rock or a water-filled jar. If you are using a small jar, just use a small weight. The weight is important to hold the cabbage down below the brine solution that forms. Cabbage that is not in the brine will spoil or soften.

One gallon glass jars of the kind that picnic quantities of pickles or mayonnaise are sold in will hold 5 pounds, or about 2 small heads of cabbage. Crocks come in many sizes, but you are most likely to find the 5-gallon size. They are large enough for 25 pounds of cabbage, or as much sauerkraut as the average family will want.

Fermenting the Cabbage: When the cabbage is packed, let it stand at room temperature (65°-72°). A lower temperature will slow down fermentation; a higher temperature can cause spoilage. Keep track of the temperature with an ordinary outdoor thermometer.

There should be enough juice from the cabbage and salt mixture to form a brine within 24 hours. If no solution is present by this time, add brine in the proportion of 1 cup of cold water to 1½ teaspoons of pickling salt. Add enough brine to cover the cabbage.

By the second or third day, air bubbles should start rising to the surface of the brine. This is the sign that fermentation has started. Each day a scum will form on the surface of the brine. Lift off the weight and cloth. Skim off the scum carefully, and wipe any scum off the insides of the container. Replace the cloth with a new sterile one and clean the plate and weight.

If the brine is so slimy that the scum won't skim off the top, it usually means the temperature is too high. It is hard to make sauerkraut when the weather is hot. The best thing to do if the brine turns slimy is to discard the sauerkraut and wait until cooler weather to try again.

Fermentation continues as long as bubbles rise to the top of the brine. When the bubbles stop, the sauerkraut is ready. Fermentation takes from two to five weeks, depending on the temperature.

This cross section shows how to pack sauerkraut. The cloth and cabbage are held beneath the brine level by the weighted plate. Scum forms at the surface of the brine. If not removed daily, accumulated scum lessens the acid content of the sauerkraut; the food will turn mushy and dark, and possibly spoil.

When fermentation is finished, the sauerkraut should be covered with a lid and placed in a very cool spot, preferably around 38°. If you have no cool spot, use the refrigerator, or process the sauerkraut.

To process the sauerkraut, heat to simmering (185°-210°). Try to avoid boiling. Pack the hot sauerkraut into clean hot jars and cover with hot juice or extra boiled water, leaving ½-inch headroom. Close the jars. Process jars in boiling water bath – 15 minutes for pints and 20 minutes for quarts.

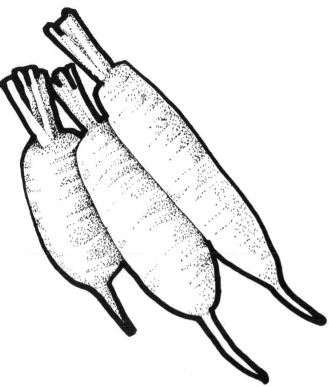

Carrots come in both short and long varieties. Which you choose depends on how deep you feel like loosening the soil.

The familiar radish is the round, red one. Less well-known, but milder in flavor, is the long white "icicle" variety.

Root Vegetables

The root crops for our garden include carrots, beets, turnips, parsnips, radishes, and salsify. If you don't have room enough in your garden for each of these vegetables, you can do a succession of plantings on the same ground to give you a root harvest that will last practically the year 'round.

Preparing the Soil

Preparation for a good root garden is a bit more troublesome than for the other vegetables in this book. It is possible, of course, just to pop the seeds into the ground and give proper watering. But your crop in that case won't be as large and the vegetables not as tasty as if you prepared the soil properly. You must be the judge as to how much time and effort you want or can afford to put into your garden.

The ground for root crops should be dug with a shovel and broken up into a loose texture with a hoe, to a depth as deep as you expect the roots to grow (the seed package will tell you the size of the mature root).

In dry, hard ground, root crops have trouble breaking through the surface. To prevent this problem, some people cover the seed of root crops with peatmoss instead of soil when planting.

Root crops are notably resistant to pests and diseases. Some people even plant radishes and turnips in between rows of tomatoes, beans and cucumbers to repel insects such as aphids and beetles.

Carrots

Carrots come in different shapes and lengths, from 3 inches to over 11 inches long. If your soil is not loose to an adequate depth, select the shorter varieties. Baby Finger Nantes is a stubby 3 inches long. Red Cored Chantenay is about 6 inches; it does well in clayey soil. Gold Pak varieties are 8 to 10 inches long, Imperator 10 to 12 inches long.

The kinds of carrots you buy in plastic packages in the supermarket, dried and with their tops cut off, are really no indication of the sweet, moist carrots that are so easy to grow in the garden.

Carrots are the one root vegetable you want to cultivate the soil deepest for, to ensure smooth, swift growth. Even if you're growing the little 3-inch types, you'll be glad you loosened the soil before planting.

Seeds should be planted in ¼ to ½-inch deep drills, ½ inch apart (in other words, sprinkled thinly). A few radish seeds along the row are helpful to mark the location of the slow-germinating carrots. Be careful not to stand on the carrot rows when you cultivate and weed, because tightly packed ground will stunt their growth. Make the rows 16 inches apart, to give yourself room to maneuver.

The carrots will sprout in two or three weeks if you keep the ground properly damp (but don't kill with kindness by soaking the ground). When the seedlings are about 2 or 3 inches high, thin them to 1½ to 2 inches apart. Carrot thinnings can be used for salads and garnishes. We advise against pulling up the tiny young carrot roots, however. Thin with scissors.

Carrots mature in about two months. Since they're good eating at all times, you can keep planting a new row every two weeks until mid-summer.

Radishes

Champion, Scarlet Globe Forcing, and Cherry Belle are good early-season varieties. Red Boy, Comet, and Red Prince Improved are fine for summer planting. Burpee White and White Icicle will produce white roots with a milder flavor than the traditional kind.

Radishes are just about the fastest and easiest plants you can grow and eat. You can have fresh red radishes in your salad three weeks after planting. Plant seeds 1½ inches apart and ½ inch deep. Rows should be 6 to 8 inches apart. If you plant seeds with this spacing, there won't be any need to thin.

Like the other root crops, radishes need good, even watering. Unlike most of the other root crops, however, they don't keep well in the ground after maturing. Harvest them as soon as they are full-grown, or the flavor will begin to spoil. The seed packet of the variety you pick will tell you how big "full-grown" is.

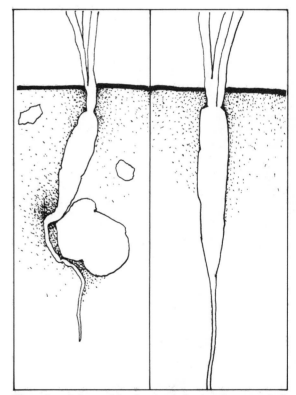

The value of deep cultivation (and clearing the ground of rocks or hard clumps of earth) is in allowing roots to develop freely and easily. Growing root crops in hard, rough ground will stunt the vegetables, as can be seen here in two carrot roots, one of which is coping with a stone.

Beets

Spring Red is good for areas where the climate is cool. Little Egypt is the quickest maturing type. Crosby's Egyptian is another early type, and Detroit Dark Red a longer maturing type suitable for winter storage.

Beet "seeds" are actually pods that contain several seeds. These pods should be planted in ½-inch-deep drills 1 inch apart. Rows of beets should be 14 inches apart. The beets will germinate within a week. Thin right away with scissors so that you have only one seedling from each of the original pods. After the seedlings are 6 inches high, thin every other one, leaving 2 inches between each plant. On the second thinning, you can pull the root and all to find that you have a small beet — good to eat. Beet greens are also good; prepare like spinach.

Beets aren't bothered much by frosts in either spring or winter. You can plant them as soon as you can dig up the ground in the spring. Lack of water, however, will hurt their growth, so in dry weather be sure not to let the ground dry out completely. Growing time will be from just over a month for "very early" varieties to almost two months. You can grow several crops of beets through the season, but a crop grown in the heat of the summer will be likely to have a "woody" taste, unless you harvest while the beets are still small and sweet. Grow a spring crop and then a fall crop planted around the first of September for root cellar storage (see page 55).

Turnips

Purple Top White Globe and Just Right are good white-fleshed varieties; Golden Ball a good yellow-fleshed variety. If you like to cook and eat turnip greens, the Seven Top variety is for you. Don't buy the varieties called "summer turnips" if you're planning to store turnips over the winter. The most popular rutabagas, the very large so-called Swedish turnips, are the Laurentian varieties.

Some people say the greens of turnips are better than the roots. Whichever you like, turnips deserve a place in your garden.

Turnips come in two kinds — one kind is called rutabaga by some people. There are loads

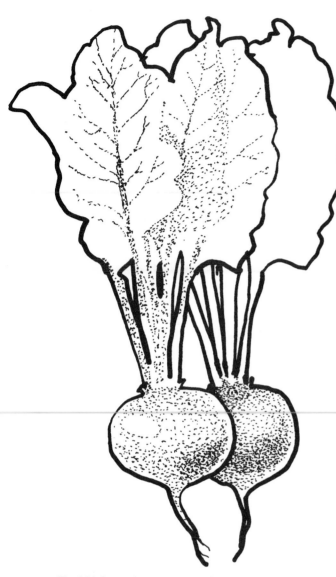

To pickle beets, choose small beets, under 3 inches. Boil until tender. Cool, peel and slice. Pack in jars, adding ½ teaspoon salt per pint. Pour equal amounts of vinegar and water in jars until beets are covered to ½ inch of top. Process after sealing in boiling water-bath for 30 minutes. Pickled beets are also good with a little sugar and a sprinkle of pickling spices added to each jar.

of sizes and colors of both kinds. Check seed catalogs or the backs of seed packets to see what is available. A familiar turnip is the one with a root ⅔ white (bottom) and ⅓ purple (top); it's about 3 inches across. Other kinds, especially rutabagas, grow up to twice that size. The greens of all are identical.

Although you can grow turnips in the spring, the varieties which are planted in mid-to-late summer and harvested before the first fall frost are best for taste and for winter storage. Turnips will mature in about two months and rutabagas in three. Both will continue growing for some time, but are tastier when small.

Sow rutabagas about a month earlier than turnips. Plant ¼ inch deep, 3 seeds to every inch of row. Rows should be 24 inches apart. Thin to 4 to 8 inches apart, depending on how big the final root will be. You might enjoy trying the thinnings in salads and stews.

Parsnips

Hollow Crown Improved, Harris Model, All American, and Guernsey are all good varieties.

Parsnips are a root crop vegetable that can be left in the ground right through the winter. Their flavor seems to improve with this kind of treatment — or maybe it's just the heightened enjoyment of eating fresh garden vegetables in the winter.

Parsnips have a long growing season — four months plus — so get them in the ground as early in the spring as you can, after the ground is crumbly rather than a melting muck.

Plant parsnips ½ inch deep in drills, ¼ inch apart. Leave 16 inches between rows. Sprouting time is about three weeks — longer if your soil is still cold, so mixing in radish seeds is a good idea here, to mark the rows. Thin the plants to 3 inches apart when the seedlings are about 2 inches tall.

If you leave some parsnips in the ground over the winter and find that they've sprouted again in the spring, don't be surprised. They're actually biennials — they take two years to reach maturity. The hitch is that after the second year's leaf growth forms, the root is no longer good for eating. So pull them all up and plant a new crop the second year.

To fix turnip greens, twist the top off and discard the hard, tough stems, keeping the leaves. Wash thoroughly in cold water. Then boil, using 6 ounces of water for each pound of greens. Simmer with a chopped onion and salt pork or ham until tender. Add salt and pepper to taste.

Vegetables like parsnips that are left in the ground over the winter will not suffer from freezing; what will injure them, however, are frequent freezes followed by thaws. They will tend to become mushy and decompose. A covering of newspapers, leaves, or grass clippings protects the roots from drastic temperature changes.

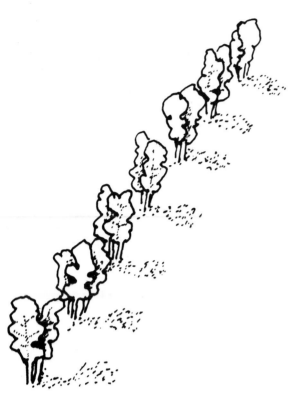

Keeping the ground free of weeds while waiting for the root crops to sprout can be a problem. The danger lies in scraping up root crop seeds or seedlings along with what you suspect are weeds. One solution is to mix radish seeds with the other root crop seeds. When the radishes sprout, in 2 or 3 days after planting, they will mark the row for you so you can avoid hoeing away your vegetables.

Salsify stew can be made by browning 1 pound ground beef and adding 1 cup diced carrot, 1 cup diced onion, 1 tablespoon chopped parsley, 1 teaspoon tarragon, 1 teaspoon marjoram. Simmer 45 minutes. Meanwhile, wash 10 salsify, twist off tops and simmer in water 15 minutes. Combine with other ingredients and simmer 45 minutes more. Serve with lemon quarters to squeeze over stew.

Salsify

Mammoth Sandwich Island is usually the only variety of salsify sold.

The growing time for salsify is a long one — 150 days from planting to harvest — which may explain their lack of availability in supermarkets. Why plant and harvest one crop of a vegetable when you can plant and harvest 2 or 3 crops of carrots in the same space? So goes the reasoning of the commercial farmer. Fortunately, you can use your own space to grow and try salsify. Most people say they taste like oysters, and in some places salsify is known as the oyster plant. We know they're delicious in a cream sauce.

Cultivation is about the same as for the other root vegetables. You'll need to loosen the soil before planting to a 6 to 8 inch depth. Plant seeds ½-inch deep in drills, dropping the tiny seeds about ¼ inch apart. When they germinate in about 2 to 3 weeks, thin to 3 inches apart, and keep moist. If you don't have 150 days of growing season, don't worry. Salsify will keep growing through several frosts, and can be harvested all winter long, whenever the ground thaws enough to dig them.

Storing Root Vegetables

With the exception of radishes, any of the root crops can be left in the ground over the winter for harvest in spring or during winter thaws. Most people, however, find that beets and turnips become less pleasantly flavored — more "woody" — when treated this way. Carrots, salsify, and especially parsnips, do well in the ground over the winter.

An old-fashioned, but easy and effective, way to preserve your root vegetables is the root cellar. This doesn't necessitate an addition onto your house. A root cellar can be an unheated garage or shed, cold section of your basement, or a device as simple as a pile of sand against a wall or fence.

The three important factors for a root cellar are: temperature, moisture, and space.

You want the temperature to be above freezing and yet cool enough to preserve the vegetables. Don't always be running out with a thermometer to check the ground temperature. If your storage area is protected from wind and insulated naturally with leaves, wood or brick, the temperature will be all right.

Enough space is needed to keep roots from touching one another, as moisture is usually provided by burying the vegetables in moist sand.

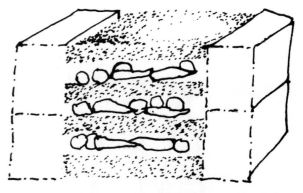

If your root cellar is a porch or unheated garage, use wooden apple boxes filled with damp sand for root storage. The simplest root cellar of all is a pile of sand held in place against a house wall or fence with concrete blocks.

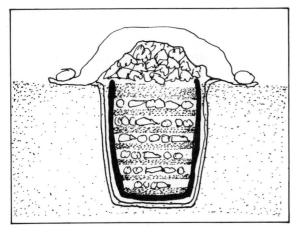

The cold frame that was described on page 24 would make an ideal root cellar. So does this barrel buried in the ground. Vegetables are kept moist by burying them in damp sand. Spread them so they do not touch, and keep 2 inches of sand between layers.

Peas and Beans

Beans — called green beans, string beans, or snap beans interchangeably — are immature pods of the same beans that at maturity are dried for use in soups, stews and baked beans. Since you grow green beans for the pod, or shell, you'll use different varieties than if you were growing for the bean inside. If you want, though, you can grow any snap beans to maturity, harvest and dry the beans. Peas, a close relative of beans, are usually eaten as immature seeds, but snow peas are eaten for the crisp pods.

Pea Varieties

Peas are primarily a spring and early summer crop in most of the country. They don't appreciate full summer heat, so you should plant as early as possible. Harvest time is in about 60 days. If you plant a second crop in early September, it is sometimes possible to get a late harvest. Fall crops may have a smaller yield of inferior quality, however, and an early frost can destroy the entire planting. If you live far enough south so that frost won't come till late November or December, a fall planting could be worthwhile.

The easiest peas to plant are the "dwarf vine" varieties. These are really bushes, 16 to 24 inches high, which need no staking. Improved Laxton's Progress, Little Marvel, and Burpees Blue Bantam are all suitable dwarf vine varieties. The taller, heavy-bearing vine types require staking. They include Miragreen, Tall Telephone, and Lincoln. The edible-pod types, sometimes called Chinese snow peas, are often used in Chinese cooking. You harvest these when the pods show very slight bumps, indicating the development of peas inside has just started. Cook them whole and enjoy a fresh crisp taste. Little Sweetie is a good bush variety of these, and Mammoth Melting Sugar a very tall vine type.

Pea Cultivation

Prepare your pea patch with an extra layer of fertilizer 6 inches below the surface. Cover with soil so the pea seeds don't come in direct contact with the fertilizer. Even if you skip the fertilizer, it's a good idea to loosen the soil with a shovel to a depth of 6 to 8 inches. Plant peas 1 inch deep in drills at 1 inch intervals, with rows 24 inches apart. Look for germination in a week or two. You won't have to thin.

If you have planted one of the tall vining types, it will be easiest to put in the stakes at the time you seed. When the seeds germinate, twigs or sticks should be thrust into the ground to support the young seedlings until they begin to climb their permanent supports. If they fall over, their growth can be stunted. Keep the soil moist. When the pea pods are about 3 inches long, check to see if the peas inside are full-size. If so, twist off the pods, being careful not to damage the vines, and cook as soon as possible to catch the fresh flavor.

Bush Bean Varieties

String beans grow on bushes or the vines are often trained to climb up poles and so are called pole beans. There are different planting and cultivating procedures for each kind. We'll take up the bush bean types here, and the pole type beans on page 58.

Good varieties of green bush beans are Spring Green, Contender, and Spartan Arrow. All mature in around 40 days and produce a 5 to 6 inch pod at picking time. Tendercrop is a slightly slower variety to mature, but its pods stay fresh longer after picking and are good for freezing because of their deep green color.

Waxbeans, the delicious yellow form of string beans, are Gold Crop, Pencil Pod Wax, and Eastern Butterwax.

Bush Bean Cultivation

Both green and wax bush beans are cultivated the same way. They are not at all tolerant of frost and germinate poorly in cold ground. Since they mature in less than 60 days, you can delay planting until conditions are absolutely safe.

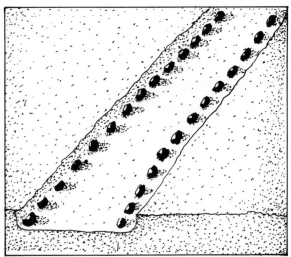

To make the best use of your space, plant peas in double rows, particularly if you are going to stake them. Wet down the soil before starting. Then make a trench 1 inch deep and 6 inches wide. Put seeds on either side of the trench at 1-inch intervals. Cover the seeds up to ground level and tamp down firmly with the back of a hoe.

The best support for pea plants, because they are spaced so closely, is a continuous row of stakes, 36 inches apart and 5 feet high. Tie strings between the stakes at intervals (beginning from the ground) 6 inches high, then 12 inches, 18 inches, and 24 inches.

Peas send out small tendrils that wind about a support to hold the plant up. Strings are good supports, but narrow sticks will work too. Don't use chicken wire – it is hard to pull the tendrils from it after harvest. String supports can be cut when you uproot the plants. If dwarf vine type plants seem to sag (especially from a heavy rain) use short twigs stuck in the ground for their tendrils to hold onto.

All beans like rich soil, and it helps to dig some compost into the ground before planting. Stronger fertilizer like manure, blood meal or chemical fertilizers, should be worked more deeply into the soil if used. The seeds should not be touching the fertilizer directly.

Plant seeds 1 to 1½ inches deep, 4 inches apart, with rows 24 inches apart. With good weather, the beans will germinate in 7 to 10 days. Keep the rows free from weeds until the plants are large enough to shade the ground.

For best flavor, pick the beans as early as possible when they are 4 to 5 inches long. When a slight twist on the pod snaps the pod off the vine, they can be picked.

If you harvest beans when they're green, they will respond by growing more pods, and you can continue harvesting from the same plants for as long as the season lasts.

Pole Bean Varieties

Pole bean varieties for growing green snap beans are numerous. By far the favorites are Ramona and Kentucky Wonder. Kentucky Wonder is available in the yellow wax variety too. Cooler weather is more suitable for the Ramona pole bean.

Dried bean varieties are many and varied; they are useful in the cooking of many different nationalities. If the following varieties are not available at your garden store, you can safely plant any beans you find in health food departments.

Our own Boston Baked Beans are made from beans of the white bean group, which includes navy beans, pea beans, and marrow beans.

Lentils are the little disc-like beans that are often used in a thick soup. They are also delicious in casseroles or by themselves.

Black or turtle beans are used in many Spanish-American style dishes. Black bean soup with a dash of sherry is a wonderful treat on a cold day.

Kidney beans are the deep red, kidney-shaped beans popular in chilis. Pink and Pinto beans are similar to the kidney bean, but different colors. They can be used in any recipes that call for kidney beans.

Chick Peas, also called garbanzos or ceci beans, are roundish, wrinkly beans that have a nut-like taste. They are used in Spanish, Italian and Middle Eastern cooking.

Lima beans are the basis for many casseroles.

Soybeans are a staple food in many parts of the world and in terms of protein value are the best of all the beans. There are many recipes for cooking soybeans, but you can substitute them in any recipe you have that calls for dried beans. Soybeans come in bush varieties too.

Split peas make wonderful soups, but they have had their skins removed in a mechanical process that is too difficult for the home gardener.

These dried beans, from left to right, are pea beans, kidney beans, chick peas, fava beans and black beans.

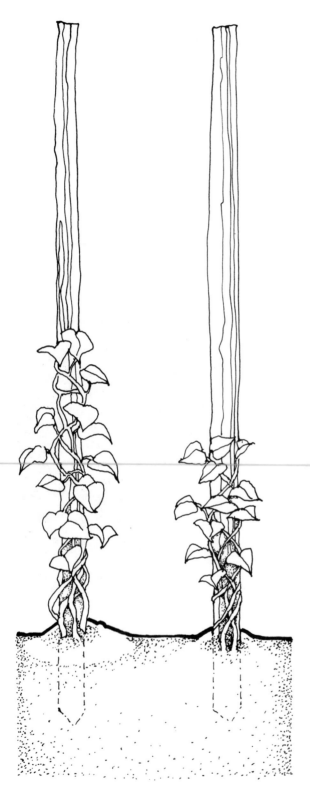

Pole Bean Cultivation

Growing dried beans of the climbing, or pole, type is practical, because of the tremendous yield that pole-type growing offers. Like Jack's beanstalk, there is almost no limit to the height of your plant, except that for you, unlike Jack, the plant will flop over when it reaches the top of its support.

About those supports — you can use just plain poles for the plants to wind around. If you can get wood poles with a rough surface, all the better to make it easier for the plants to climb. The poles should be at least 5 feet high — higher if you can manage it — and 2 inches in diameter. Thicker diameter poles are fine, but thinner ones are liable not to last through the season. A fence-type support can be as simple as the one described for peas on page 57, except that you should use at least 5 or 6 horizontal wires or good strong twine to accommodate the greater height and weight of climbing beans. You can also use poles to support a fence of chicken wire, plastic mesh, or other durable support.

Drive poles at least $1/10$ of their height into the ground for good support. A good way to drive poles is to make a hole with a crowbar or tirejack. The pole will still fit snugly, but you won't risk splitting it as you drive it into the ground. Drive the poles into the ground 30

The plants in this hill of beans will grow to the full 6 foot height of the pole, and even higher if the growing season is long. Poles are 30 inches apart. You can plant somewhat more bean plants by using a tall chicken wire or similar fence support, since the plants can be 6 inches apart along the whole length of the fence.

inches apart. Set the rows 36 inches apart.

If you use poles you will plant a "hill" of beans at the base of each. With a shovel, loosen a circle of earth about a foot in diameter to a depth of 10 inches. Break up clods. Set 6 beans in a small circle on the surface, placing them 1 inch apart. Poke a hole in the earth with your finger, about 1½ inches deep, for each seed. Cover with soil and tamp down the entire circle lightly.

Look for sprouting to start about a week after you plant. When the beans sprout and the seedlings are 3 to 4 inches high, thin each hill to the strongest 3 or 4 plants.

If you use a long fence or wire as a support for your bean stalks, plant one seed every 6 inches along the support. You won't need to thin these. Rows of beans planted this way can be 30 inches apart.

Like the bush beans, pole beans should not be planted until the ground has thoroughly warmed up. This will mean late May or early June most places. Most dried beans take over three months from planting to maturity. Pole-type green beans can be harvested in two months.

Bean And Pea Pests

Prevention is the best defense against bean and pea pests and diseases. Use disease-resistant varieties if you can. Plant beans or peas in a different spot each year. To avoid spreading fungus diseases, don't move around the bean or pea patch when the leaves are wet from rain or a watering. If you can water the beans only at the base of the plants, instead of sprinkling the entire plant, do it.

If the leaves of the bean plants yellow early in the season, you may be the victim of leafhoppers, particularly if flower buds drop as well. These insects are hard to spot, because of their habit of quickly skipping away. Dusting with rotenone may be necessary. Yellow leaves on plants that are bearing pods is only a normal sign of old age.

Bean beetles, another common pest, are round little crawlers with eight spots on either side of their backs. Pick them off and kill them. Remove their orange-colored egg clusters from the undersides of leaves.

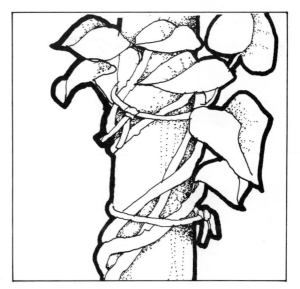

If you have used smooth poles for support, and the beans show a reluctance to climb, help them along by twining them counter clockwise around the pole or support and tying them as lightly as possible with string or twist-ties. Similarly, with a fence or supporting wires, show your beans the way and tie them up where they belong.

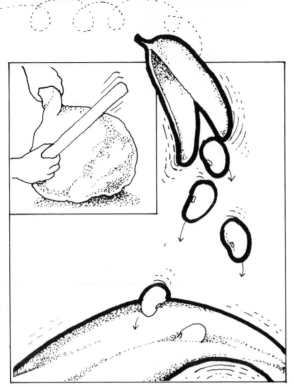

One way of shelling beans is to collect them in a sheet on a windy day, gather up the four corners to make a bundle, and beat the bundles with a stick to break the dry pods. When they are well broken, get friends (or family) to hold on to the four sheet corners and toss the beans until the wind has blown most of the dry pods away, leaving the beans in the sheet.

To cook dried beans, wash them in cold water and soak for at least 8 hours (or overnight) in water three times the volume of the beans. Lentils need no soaking. Cook beans in the water they were soaking in, adding more water to cover if necessary. Bring beans and water to a boil, reduce heat, and simmer for ½ to 2 hours (depending on size of beans), or until tender. To test "doneness," blow on a bean in a spoon. If the skin cracks, the beans are done.

Drying Beans

When you allow bean pods to mature on the plant, as you must for dried beans, the plant will produce no more beans. This is why the pole beans, with their larger yields, are suitable for the home gardener who has space for only a few plants.

When your beans have fully matured on the plant, the pods will be dry and crack open easily. At this stage, pull the entire plant out of the ground. Pull off the bean pods and collect them. The rest of the plant should be thrown on your compost heap or disposed of. This keeps insects and disease from gaining a foothold from one year to the next. Take the bean pods and store them in a dry, protected place like a dry basement or garage for a week or so. Then shell the beans. Bean weevils may have laid their eggs among the beans while on the plant, so if you plan to store the beans after drying, you should treat them by heating them in a shallow pan in an oven set at 130° for 30 minutes. Store in jars.

Dried Bean Recipes

Baked Beans

Baked beans is a dish which is both filling and nutritious. You can use any dried beans in this recipe but the baked beans familiar to most Americans are white pea or navy beans.

Put 1½ cups of dry beans in 5 cups of water and let soak overnight. If any beans are floating on the top in the morning, remove them. Cook, simmering in their own water until tender, about ½ hour. Drain and remove from the pot, reserving the bean water.

Preheat the oven to 275° and add the following ingredients in a large crock or casserole:

the cooked beans	2 tablespoons
1 teaspoon salt	molasses
2 tablespoons catsup	1 teaspoon dry
(optional)	mustard
1 small onion studded	½ cup boiling bean
with 3 cloves	water
	¼ pound salt pork

Cover the pot and bake at least 4 hours. Don't

worry about over-cooking; it's almost impossible. Check periodically to see that the beans are not dry. If they appear to be, add more water. Cook uncovered for the last half hour.

Bean Stew with Lamb

3 pounds lean lamb, cubed	½ cup chopped mint leaves
3 cups cooked kidney beans	3 lemons
1 cup chopped parsley	16 chopped scallions
	6 tablespoons butter salt and pepper to taste

In a heavy 4-quart pot heat 4 tablespoons butter, scallions, and parsley. Cook until the parsley is deep green. Heat the rest of the butter in a skillet and brown the meat. Combine meat and mint with the cooked scallions and parsley. Add water to cover, along with the juice of the lemons. Cover and simmer 1 to 1½ hours, or until the meat is almost tender. Add the beans, and salt and pepper to taste. Continue cooking until the meat is tender. Serve over rice.

Black Bean Soup

2 cups black beans ham bone	1 bay leaf
½ cup chopped carrots	½ cup heavy cream salt and pepper
1 onion studded with 3 cloves	few grains cayenne pepper
2 stalks celery	sherry to taste

Soak the black beans in water overnight. In a large pot or kettle, put the ham bone (or pork butt, cooked ham, or bacon), drained beans, carrots, onion, celery and bay leaf with 2 to 3 quarts of water. Bring to a boil, then lower the heat and let the soup simmer until the beans are soft and mushy. This should take about three hours. Remove the ham bone and bay leaf and put the soup through a sieve, food mill, or electric blender. Add salt, pepper, and cayenne pepper to taste. Add the cream and return the soup to the stove. Bring to a boil. Serve with a tablespoon of sherry per cup. Garnish with a slice of lemon or slice of hard-boiled egg.

Humus is a Middle Eastern dish that makes a great dip. Soak garbanzo beans (chick peas) overnight in water. Drain. Cover with fresh water and boil till soft. Mash or put in a blender with sesame or olive oil, lemon juice, crushed garlic cloves, and salt to taste. Sprinkle with parsley. Serve with flat loaves of pita bread.

Bean Salad is a good summer dish. Combine 2½ cups cooked dried beans with ½ cup French dressing and chill. For a little added zest, try mixing in chopped pickles or a pinch of curry powder, or garlic.

These summer squashes, all growing on bush-type plants, are, from top to bottom, zucchini, crookneck, straightneck, and scallop.

Squash

There are many shapes, kinds and colors of squash. The different flavors and uses of squash make the selection you plant depend on what you and your family like to eat.

There are both bush and vine type squashes, and winter and summer varieties. In general, summer squash are sold as bush varieties; winter squash as vine varieties. The summer squash varieties grow from seed to maturity in about two months, the winter squash in three months. Summer squash have more water in them than the winter varieties and cannot be stored. Winter squash, on the other hand, requires more space to grow. The plants and fruits are bigger and tend to sprawl. Winter squash may need some staking to protect the fruit from lying on the ground.

Summer Squash Varieties

Taking the last (alphabetically) first, zucchini is probably the most popular squash variety in the United States. Zucchini resembles a cucumber in size, shape and color. Some zucchini are yellow or grayish green, but the dark green kind remains the favorite. They are generally cucumber color inside. All are summer bush types. Cocozelle, also called Italian marrow, is similar to zucchini, but is lighter green. Crookneck and straightneck look like haughty geese with green bills (stem) and creamy yellow bodies. Both grow almost a foot long, but are tastier when 4 to 6 inches. White Patty Pan and St. Pat Scallop resemble small, full pies. One is white, the other green.

Summer Squash Cultivation

All the summer squash mature in less than 60 days. Sow them after the soil has warmed up in late May or early June. Sow ½ inch deep in hills, with 6 seeds per each 1 foot hill. Hills should be spaced 3 feet apart and rows 4 feet apart. Remember that squash bushes will produce heavily. Thin each hill to 3 or 4 plants after the first true leaves have formed. Staking is not necessary. Keep the plants well watered, and cultivate the soil often to keep the weeds from getting a start. If weeds get established and you try to dig them out you will run the risk of damaging the shallow squash roots.

Squash can be picked any time after the blossom drops off the end of the fruit. Keep picking off fruit before it matures completely in order to keep your plants producing more fruit. Summer squash is ready to eat as long as you can poke a fingernail easily through its skin. If the skin is tougher than that, pick off the fruit and throw it away.

Winter Squash Varieties

Winter squash varieties include hubbard, butternut, acorn (Table Queen), and buttercup. Acorn and butternut mature in about three months time; buttercup in 15 weeks; and hubbard in four months. Both buttercup and hubbard types can be picked early and cooked like summer squash. The others should be ripened fully. When mature, all the winter squash plants are much bigger than the summer varieties, and will need much more space in your garden.

Winter Squash Cultivation

When night temperatures no longer go below 50° in the spring you can plant winter squash. Plant seed ½ inch deep in hills of 6 to 8 seeds. Hills should be 8 feet apart, as should the rows. (But before planting more than a few hills of squash, ask yourself: What am I going to do with all this squash?) Plants don't have to be staked, but you may find it helpful to build a support for the heavy fruit, to be sure of keeping them from rotting on the ground. See page 41 for a chicken wire support. Water well, trying to keep the water at the base of the plant and not on the leaves.

Squash Pests

Keep an eye out for the cucumber beetle (stripes on back) or squash beetle (spots on back). Both of these characters lay yellow or orange egg clusters on the bottom side of the squash leaves. Larvae that hatch from these love to lunch on squash leaves. Pick off the adult bugs early in the morning while they're not so active; pluck off any leaves that harbor egg clusters.

These winter squashes, from top to bottom, are butternut, acorn and hubbard.

Storing Winter Squash

Winter squash must fully mature on the vine if you are planning to harvest it for storage. The skin should be as hard as possible — test by trying to pierce it with your fingernail. Pick the fruit before the first hard frost. Cut it off the vine with a knife leaving part of the stem on the fruit. If you have a mild Indian summer day or two, let the squash "cure" in the warm sun. Otherwise, store it for a week in a warm room indoors. Then move it to a cool basement or porch where the temperature will stay between 45° and 65°. Check fruit in about a month. Any that were not mature when picked will have begun to turn soft. Remove and discard them. The others should be good for several months. Acorn squash will not last as long as some other varieties of winter squash, so eat it first.

Squash Recipes

Ratatouille

Summer squash is not particularly rewarding either frozen or canned. Instead, a good way to preserve it is in the spicy vegetable dish called ratatouille, which if made in quantity is excellent either preserved or frozen.

Note: Detailed information for preserving foods safely by boiling water-bath, hot water-bath and steam-pressure methods will be found on pages 74 and 75.

4 tablespoons butter	1 medium green pepper, seeded and cut into strips
1 medium eggplant, peeled and cubed	1 large onion, chopped
1 medium zucchini, cubed	1 garlic clove, crushed
6 medium tomatoes, peeled and cut into eighths	1 tablespoon parsley, chopped
	salt and pepper

Combine all the ingredients except the salt and pepper. Simmer 20 minutes or until tender, then salt and pepper to taste. Pour into freezer containers. The mixture can now be frozen until needed at a later date; or canned in a pressure canner at 10 pounds pressure, 30 minutes for pints, 40 minutes for quarts.

Strained Winter Squash

Although winter squash stores well, it is convenient to have quarts of cooked, strained squash on hand for baking.

You can store strained squash for use in squash bread or squash pie, or as a slightly sweet starchy vegetable similar to mashed sweet potato or yam.

Wash the squash and prepare by scraping out the seeds and cutting into uniform pieces. Bake covered in a 350° oven until tender. Scrape pulp from the skin with a spoon and put through a food mill. Pack into jars, leaving ¾-inch headspace. Process in pressure canner at 10 pounds pressure, 65 minutes for pints, 80 minutes for quarts.

Squash Bread

1 cup strained winter squash	¼ teaspoon baking soda
1½ cups sugar	¾ teaspoon salt
½ cup butter or margarine	⅓ teaspoon cinnamon
2 eggs	½ teaspoon cloves
1⅔ cups flour	½ teaspoon nutmeg
	½ cup chopped nuts (optional)

Mix softened butter, sugar, and eggs together. Sift the dry ingredients together and add to the sugar mixture. Stir in the squash and nuts. Pour into two greased bread pans and bake in a 350° oven for 1½ hours. Cool on a rack.

Squash Pie

1½ cups strained winter squash	1 teaspoon cinnamon
1½ cups heavy cream	½ teaspoon cloves
½ cup brown sugar	a pinch of nutmeg
¼ cup white sugar	4 slightly beaten eggs
½ teaspoon salt	1 teaspoon vanilla
	2 tablespoons brandy

Mix all the ingredients together in the top half of a double boiler. Cook, stirring, over hot water until thick. Cool slightly and add 1 teaspoon of vanilla or 2 tablespoons of brandy. Pour the mixture into a baked pie shell. Let firm. This pie is particularly good with whipped cream.

Squash Pancakes aren't familiar to many people. You might like to try them. Mix together 2 cups cooked mashed squash, 2 tablespoons honey, 1 cup flour, and ¼ cup milk. Add more milk or flour to bring the thickness of the mixture to pancake batter consistency. Drop spoonfuls in hot butter in a skillet to make the cakes. Fry until golden.

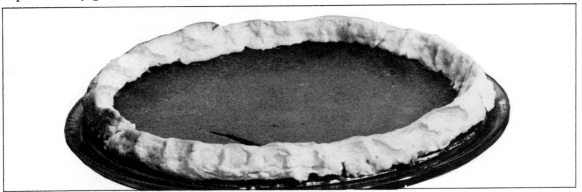

Other Favorites

There are many other fruits and vegetables besides the ones in this book that you may want to plant in your home garden. Your choice will depend on your family's likes and dislikes, how much room you have for planting, and how important preserving and storage are to you. We have included the following ones because, although they are not the most efficient or economical, they are all very popular crops.

Corn

Corn is very rewarding to grow at home for those who love it, because the sooner it is eaten after being picked, the better it tastes.

Early Sunglow is a good early yellow variety; ears will be about 7 inches long. Burpee's Honeycross and Seneca Chief are 8 to 9 inches long and take about 90 days to grow; both are yellow varieties.

Stagger the planting of corn over a period of several weeks, so you will have a steady harvest later. Plant corn after the last frost in late spring in hills of 3 seeds, 30 inches between hills. Rows should be 30 inches apart.

Asparagus

Martha Washington is the standard asparagus variety. Asparagus is a perennial which will keep producing every spring for years. Unfortunately, if you start it from seed, it won't reach maturity for three years.

If you're eager for asparagus, you can buy one-year-old roots for about 20¢ apiece. Two-year-old roots do not transplant well, so you can't have asparagus for eating your first year, no matter what you do.

If you buy seeds plant them thinly in shallow drills that are 30 inches apart, and thin to 3 inches apart the first year, picking out inferior plants for thinning until the ones left by the third year are a foot apart.

If you buy roots, plant in the spring, after the last frost.

Keep asparagus well watered. After the leafy foliage has turned brown in the fall or early winter, the stem of the plant should be cut off at ground level. Follow this pruning procedure each year.

Most gardeners plant more than one row of corn to encourage pollination of the ears. The top of the stalk will blossom with pollen stalks. The pollen must reach the tassels at the end of each ear, farther down the plant, or the ears will not develop.

In the third year of the plant's life, cut spears for harvest when they are over 5 inches long. Don't cut closer than 2 inches from the ground, so that new shoots can develop.

Eggplant And Peppers

Both eggplant and peppers can be grown in the same way as tomatoes. In fact, starting plants indoors in pots or flats may be a necessity with eggplant and peppers because they take a long time to mature. If you set out eggplants that have been growing indoors for 8 weeks, you will still have to have 2½ months of warm weather before you can harvest the eggplant fruit. The night temperature for eggplants outdoors should be above 55°.

Black Beauty and Jersey King are good eggplant varieties. Plant seeds ½ inch deep. If you start the seeds in flats or pots, you will have to transplant each seedling to a 4-inch pot about a month after they germinate.

Peppers may take even longer to grow than eggplants. Start peppers indoors 9 weeks before you expect the last frost in the spring. Sweet peppers include California Wonder (a good size for stuffing) and Sweet Banana, which changes color from green to yellow to a mature red. Hungarian Wax, Large Cherry, and Long Red Cayenne are hot pepper types.

Strawberries

Strawberry plants can be purchased for from 15 to 35¢ apiece. They come in two types — "June-bearing" and "everbearing." June-bearing is the most common type. Plant them in early spring. Everbearing actually give two or more crops. If you plant them in the fall, you will have a crop the following summer and again that fall.

Set the plants out in holes dug 8 inches deep and 24 inches apart. Rows should be 36 inches apart. Every third year, a new crop should be planted.

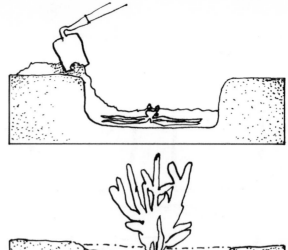

To plant asparagus, dig a foot-wide hole about 10 inches deep for each plant. Spread the roots out, keeping the buds pointed upward. Fill in around and over the roots until all but the buds at the center of the plant are covered. Leave about 6 inches of space between the top of the plant and the top of the hole. As the plant grows and sends out new roots over the season, cover them as they appear, always leaving the top of the plant exposed.

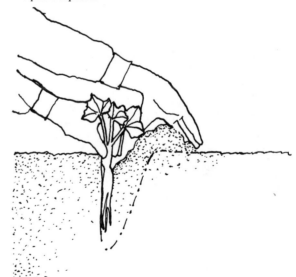

The depth of planting strawberries is important. Set the plant in at about the midpoint of its crown. The crown is the top of the root, from which green branches are growing. Most gardeners pinch all the first year's blossoms off June-bearing plants as soon as they appear the first year. This gives the plant time to gather its strength for full-size, rather than puny, berries by its second and third year. This is not necessary on everbearing types.

Airtight, rigid containers made of polyethylene are most often used for cut-up food or food packed in liquid. Houseware stores offer a variety of different shapes and sizes. Square shapes pack most efficiently. All are re-usable.

Flexible polyethylene bags are used for products with irregular shapes that are packed without syrup, such as berries and string beans. Insert the food, press out the air with your fingers, and seal by twisting the top of the bag tightly and tying with the wire ties that come with the freezer bags.

After preparing your food, pack it firmly to eliminate as much air as possible. When the foods are packed in liquid, leave about ½-inch headspace in a pint container, and 1 inch in a quart to allow for expansion as the liquid freezes. When packing the food dry, only ½-inch space is needed in any container.

Freezing

Foods that are frozen taste closer to fresh than any other kind of preserved food. Frozen foods also retain their nutrients well. The process of freezing is much less fussy than canning, and many foods can be successfully frozen that cannot be canned or preserved by other methods. Freezing preserves food by stopping the growth of organisms within the food. When the food is defrosted, this growth continues, which is why people are encouraged to use defrosted food promptly.

Freezing Equipment

The initial investment for a freezer is high, so you will want to consider it carefully. Shop around for one that meets your space needs. Six cubic feet of freezing space for each person in your family is a good rule of thumb. A cubic foot will hold about 35 pounds of food. An upright freezer is more convenient for packing and for finding what you have packed, but when you open it, cold air, which is heavier than the surrounding air, literally falls out. A chest-type freezer may be harder to find things in, but the cold air stays in when it is opened making it both safer and more efficient. For maintaining already-frozen food, the temperature regulator is set to between 0 and minus 5°. To freeze fresh food, a lower temperature of minus 20° is advisable. For freezing you must use containers that will prevent moisture from escaping or excess air from reaching the food. The usual choice is plastic bags or boxes.

Preparing Vegetables For Freezing

Freezing is effective for most vegetables. Don't try to freeze salad greens, tomatoes, Irish potatoes, green onions, or radishes, all of which become mushy when frozen. Always try to pick young, tender vegetables and freeze them as soon as they are packed. The less time from garden to freezer, the greater the nutritive value and the flavor retained.

Vegetables require blanching before they are frozen. Blanching cleanses the surface of the vegetable, brightens the color, and deactivates the enzymes which cause deterioration during storage. The best way to blanch vegetables is to boil them briefly. Boil one pound of vegetables per gallon of water.

After you have boiled the vegetables the proper amount of time, drain them and run cold water over them until there is no warmth left in them. This stops the cooking process so you do not overcook the food. The cooling process generally takes about the same amount of time as the boiling process. Drain the vegetables and pack into clean containers, seal tightly, label, and place them in the freezer. When you want to use the vegetables, add as little water as possible and cook to the desired consistency.

Preparing Fruits For Freezing

As with vegetables, the best frozen fruits are those picked at the peak of their flavor. Never freeze overripe fruit. Select fruit carefully, cutting out bad spots. Wash and peel or slice as you would fresh. Use stainless steel utensils, since iron causes many fruits to darken. In the case of apples, peaches, or pears, exposure to air can also cause darkening. To avoid this, dissolve a teaspoon of ascorbic acid (vitamin C) or a tablespoon of citric acid into a gallon of water. Drop the fruit into this solution as soon as it is peeled.

Frozen fruit can be packed three ways — in sugar syrup, in powdered sugar, or unsweetened. For the sugar syrup, dissolve granulated sugar in boiling water and let cool to 70° or less. How sweet you make the syrup is a matter of taste. Fill the container about ⅓ full with syrup. Pack the fruit to within ½ inch for a pint or 1 inch for a quart container. Then add enough syrup to cover the fruit. Crush a piece of plastic film and press down on the fruit to keep it from floating to the top before closing the container.

For the powdered sugar pack, mix the fruit together with the powdered sugar, to taste. Stir, but try to avoid crushing the fruit. Pack in either rigid containers or bags.

Freezer Storage Life	
Product	Length of Storage (in months)
citrus fruits	3 to 4
other fruits	12
spaghetti sauce (with meat)	3 to 4
onions	3 to 6
corn on the cob	8 to 10
other vegetables	12
cooked vegetables	3 to 4

Blanching Times for Frozen Vegetables	
snap beans	3 minutes
asparagus	3 minutes (for large spears)
beets	cook until tender
broccoli	3 minutes
cabbage (wedges)	3 minutes
carrots (whole)	5 minutes
corn on the cob	8 minutes
corn (cut)	5-6 minutes
eggplant	4 minutes
peas	2 minutes
summer squash	3 minutes
winter squash	cook until tender

In the unsweetened pack, place the prepared fruit directly in containers or bags. This method is recommended for figs, gooseberries, cranberries, currants, or rhubarb. Most other fruits, however, are better prepared with either the syrup or powdered sugar.

Fruits And Vegetables

Freezing does not improve ingredients so freeze only your best quality produce. Clean the food and containers carefully.

After packing your food, be sure to label each package with masking tape. The label should include not only an identification of the contents, but the date the package was frozen. Frozen food cannot be left indefinitely. Keep an inventory of what you have in the freezer. Put those products with a short freezer life toward the front where you can more easily keep track of them.

The quicker your food is frozen, the more flavor it will retain. Place food to be frozen directly against the freezer plates or coils. Leave a little space between the packages and don't try to freeze too much at once. You should not try to freeze more than 2 or 3 pounds per cubic foot of space in the freezer. The food will be frozen after 24 hours and can then be stacked more closely.

Syrups For Freezing Fruits		
Type of Syrup	Sugar/ 1 Qt. Water	Yield/ of Syrup
light	2 cups	5 cups
medium	3 cups	5½ cups
heavy	4¾ cups	6½ cups

medium with corn syrup: use 1½ cups sugar, 1 cup corn syrup to 3 cups water.

medium with honey: use 1 cup sugar, 1 cup honey to 4 cups water.

Relative Acidity of Fruits and Vegetables	
STRONG ACID: Process at 212° F. in boiling water-bath	plums
	prunes
	apricots
	apples, blackberries
	sour cherries
	peaches
	sauerkraut
	sweet cherries
	pears
WEAK ACID: Process at 240° F. in steam-pressure canner	pumpkins, carrots
	cabbage, turnips
	beets, string beans
	spinach
	asparagus, cauliflower
	lima beans
	peas
	corn

The pH (acid) chart above indicates which vegetables and fruits can be processed in a boiling water-bath, and which need steam-pressure canning.

Canning

Foods are canned in two ways. Those foods that are high in acid content such as fruits, tomatoes, sauerkraut, and pickled vegetables are processed in a boiling water-bath. Or, in the case of jams and jellies, very hot water. This means that the jars of food are cooked in boiling water for a specified amount of time. The combination of acid and heat is enough to destroy the tiny organisms that might spoil the food, or cause food poisoning. High-acid fruits and vegetables are safer to can than low-acid vegetables.

But most vegetables have a low acid content. *Therefore, to safely process these in a reasonable length of time, it is necessary to cook them under pressure at a temperature of 240° in order to ensure the killing of harmful bacteria.* This is called the "pressure method" of processing. Great care must be taken to process low acid foods according to instructions and for the amount of time indicated for the particular fruit or vegetable. Improper home canning has resulted in the tragedy of death from botulism, a toxic poisoning caused by bacterial growth in canned foods.

Canning Equipment

The boiling water-bath container for high acid foods can be any kettle that is deep enough to hold the jars. But for canning low-acid vegetables, you will need a steam pressure canner. This is not the same as a pressure cooker. Most pressure cookers are too small and lack adequate pressure control. A pressure canner is a heavy kettle with a cover which can be locked down to make it steam tight. The cover has a safety valve, a vent called a petcock with a pressure gauge to permit accurate control of temperature.

A steam pressure canner is an expensive investment, so if you buy one get a model deep enough to use as a boiling water-bath container too.

With the self-sealing screw-top jar, the sealing disk is placed on the jar and the metal screw band is screwed down over it. With the wire bail jar, the rubber ring is used to seal the glass lid, and the wire bail is clamped over the top. The smaller wire goes down on the body of the jar.

Altitude Chart

Water-Bath Canner	Increase processing time if the time called for is:	
altitude	20 minutes or less	more than 20 minutes
1,000 feet	1 minute	2 minutes
2,000 feet	2 minutes	4 minutes
3,000 feet	3 minutes	6 minutes
4,000 feet	4 minutes	8 minutes
5,000 feet	5 minutes	10 minutes
6,000 feet	6 minutes	12 minutes
7,000 feet	7 minutes	14 minutes
8,000 feet	8 minutes	16 minutes
9,000 feet	9 minutes	18 minutes
10,000 feet	10 minutes	20 minutes

Steam-Pressure Canner	
altitude	process at pressure of:
2,000- 3,000 feet	11½ pounds
3,000- 4,000 feet	12 pounds
4,000- 5,000 feet	12½ pounds
5,000- 6,000 feet	13 pounds
6,000- 7,000 feet	13½ pounds
7,000- 8,000 feet	14 pounds
8,000- 9,000 feet	14½ pounds
9,000-10,000 feet	15 pounds

Preparing Fruits And Vegetables For Canning

There are two methods of preparing food for the pressure canner or boiling water-bath. In both methods, the fruit or vegetable is first cleaned, peeled, and stemmed. If you like, it can be chopped or sliced at this point to make it easier to fit into the jars. Add seasoning, if any, at this time.

In the raw or cold pack method, the food is now packed immediately into the jars. Boiling water or sugar syrup is added to fill the jars.

In the hot pack method, the food is precooked before being packed into the jars. The advantage of precooking is that the food becomes more pliable and so permits a more solid pack.

Packing The Fruits And Vegetables

Check all jars carefully for any nicks or scratches on the rim that would prevent a seal. Clean all containers and jars in soapy water. Rinse and cover with clear hot water. Taking one jar at a time out of the water, pack your food firmly making sure that it is covered with liquid (boiling water or the water you have used to cook the vegetable, or sugar syrup for fruit). If the food is not covered it will discolor. To prevent the food from floating to the top and coming into contact with air, you can add crushed plastic film to the top of the jar to hold the food down.

A small space is left between the liquid and the top of the jar. It is called headspace and varies with the kind of food being packed.

Make certain that the seal (the rubbery compound inside the lid) is clean, so that it makes complete contact with the jar rim. Cover each jar as it is filled.

Processing The Fruits And Vegetables

The processing time for cold packed foods is usually longer than for hot. If you are pressure canning, the times for both hot and cold pack will be about the same. The only exception to this is summer squash, which takes longer to pressure can after being hot packed, because the density increases with cooking.

Low-Acid Vegetables: Pour 2 to 3 inches of boiling water into the canner before lowering the rack of filled jars. Tighten the cover but leave the vent open to allow steam to escape for 10 minutes or more. Then close the vent. When the pressure reaches 10 pounds as recorded on the gauge, start timing. If you live above sea level the pressure required will be different. (See altitude chart). In order to maintain a constant pressure, keep adjusting the heat under the canner.

As soon as the processing time is completed remove the canner from the stove but DO NOT OPEN IT. Let it cool until the pressure drops. When the gauge records zero, wait a few minutes and then open slowly. Make sure that the vent is pointed away from you. Then slowly remove the cover. Lift out the jars and let cool. Check the seals and store.

High-Acid Fruits and Vegetables: Place the packed jars in the rack of the canning kettle. Pour in water to cover the jars, but leave about 2 inches above the top of the water to allow boiling space. Cover and bring to a boil. When the water boils, time the process according to the boiling water-bath chart.

Testing the Seal: After the processing is finished, remove the jars from the rack or kettle and let them cool. Leave a small space between the jars so that the air can circulate freely. When the jars are cool test the seal. For metal screw tops, press down on the center of the cap. If it is already slightly concave or if it stays down when pressed, the seal is good. If you wish you can safely remove the metal band to make the jar easier to open later. If you are using a wire bail jar, test by trying to lift the glass top. If it is on tightly, the seal is safe and you may move the wire bail into place. If a jar is not sealed tightly, put it in the refrigerator and eat it as soon as possible. Or, you can empty the jar, repack it, and reprocess. Label jars with contents, date, and store.

Before using canned foods examine the cap. If the lid is bulging or the top is loose the food is not safe to eat. Throw it out and make sure no animals or children can get to it.

Canning Time Reference
For Water-Bath Canner

		Water-Bath (212°) Processing Time In Minutes		
fruits	type pack	½ pint	pints	1½ pints & quarts
apples	hot	15	20	20
applesauce	hot	15	20	20
apricots	raw	20	25	30
apricots	hot	15	20	25
berries	raw	10	15	20
berries	hot	10	10	15
cherries	raw	15	20	25
cherries	hot	10	10	15
grapes	raw	10	15	20
mixed fruits	hot	15	20	25
peaches	raw	20	25	30
peaches	hot	15	20	25
pears	hot	15	20	25
plums	hot	15	20	25

Canning Time Reference

low-acid vegetables	type pack	Steam Pressure Canner (240°) 10 Pounds Pressure Processing Time In Minutes	
		½-pints & pints	1½-pints & quarts
asparagus	raw or hot	25	30
beans, green or wax	raw or hot	20	25
beans, lima & butter	raw or hot	40	50
beets	hot	30	35
broccoli	hot	30	35
brussels sprouts	hot	30	35
cabbage	hot	30	35
carrots	raw or hot	25	30
cauliflower	hot	30	35
corn, whole-kernel	raw or hot	55	85
eggplant	hot	30	40
greens (all kinds)	hot	70	90
mixed vegetables	hot	length of time needed for vegetable requiring longest processing time	
peas	raw or hot	40	40
squash, summer	hot	30	40
squash, winter	hot	65	80

Salad Greens

Lettuce doesn't store well, except for a week or so in the refrigerator, but the crispness and nutritional value of home-grown lettuce just can't be matched by the supermarket variety. You can grow the familiar tight-head lettuce, some looser-headed varieties, leaf lettuce and Romaine lettuce. Endive, valued for its slightly bitter flavor, is not strictly a lettuce plant, but is used like lettuce and is grown in much the same way.

Lettuce Varieties

The "crisp head" lettuce varieties include the familiar "head lettuce," green outside and white or creamy yellow inside. Great Lakes and Iceberg are the most common varieties. Both require a long season of close to 3 months from seedling to maturity.

Leaf lettuce types are the easiest to grow in the home garden. (Some seed catalogs call these "loose head" types.) They have better flavor than head lettuce, too, and if they were easy to ship they'd be more often found in the

Down south, people know about mustard greens, but they are seldom grown up north. That's a surprise, because, like lettuce, mustard greens don't cotton to hot summer weather. Most seed companies carry the seeds. Grow the same way as lettuce. Ford-hook Fancy and Tendergreen are two good varieties. Mustard greens can be harvested in around 40 days, or when the edges of the leaves start to turn reddish-brown. Serve raw in salads or prepare like cooked spinach. Collards, another "southern" green, can only be grown in hot climates. But do try spinach, which is grown like lettuce except that it "bolts" easily and must be harvested before the really hot summer days. Swiss chard is grown like beets. Thin to 6 inches.

neighborhood supermarket. Green Ice is one of the best varieties for salad, with its attractive wavy, glossy green leaves. Salad Bowl looks definitely frilly. Bronze Oak Leaf and Ruby are spectacular in salads because of the bronze and red colors of the leaves. Leaf lettuce varieties mature in about half the time of the crisp-head varieties — between 40 and 50 days.

The "Butterhead" varieties take about 80 days from planting to maturity and include some of the best tasting, most elegant varieties. Bibb, Buttercrunch, Boston, Fordhook and Deer Tongue are all rewarding to the home gardener.

Romaine, or Cos, lettuce grows to what is technically a "head," but looks more like a long bunch of leaves. Get a variety that does not need to be tied for blanching, like Paris White. Romaine matures in three months.

The standard variety of endive is Green Curled, which matures in three months. Endive needs more room to grow than lettuce. After the final thinning, your plants should be 18 inches apart.

Lettuce Cultivation

Lettuce plants like cool weather. The danger in hot weather is that lettuce will "bolt," or send out a seed stalk from the center of the plant. Lettuce is more difficult to germinate in hot weather too. In most areas of the country, you can sow lettuce seed right after the last frost, keep on sowing every two weeks until June — or even later in the coolest zones. Then in September, when the weather cools, you can sow some more for fall harvest. If your family demands fresh lettuce all summer long, plant in a shady spot, keep well watered and maybe you'll get some mid-summer lettuce, particularly of the leaf types.

When planting lettuce, plant in ½-inch deep drills, dropping seeds about 3 inches apart. Rows should be 18 inches apart. Don't be in any hurry to thin, because the thinnings are good to eat, so you can let them grow for a while. Your final thinning should leave the leaf and small head lettuce plants 9 inches apart; if you are growing the crisp-head lettuce, the heads will need 12 inches of room to grow.

Keep the lettuce patch well watered, especially as the weather warms up.

Growing onions from seeds takes up to four or five months, so most home gardeners buy onion "sets," which are the baby onion bulbs, ready to be buried in early spring, 2 inches deep, 4 inches apart, in rows 12 inches apart. For full size onions harvest in three months. Onions will store in a basement or cool closet for a long time.

Garlic also comes in "sets." If you buy a garlic bulb at the grocery, and break it into cloves, each clove is a set. Plant cloves 1 inch deep and 6 inches apart in the early spring. In the fall, the foliage that grows over the clove will begin to die down. When it has wilted, dig up the garlic bulbs, which will keep the same way as onions.

Herbs

The herbs described in this book were chosen for their value in cooking. They are the ones most widely used in a variety of dishes, and can easily be substituted for other herbs in recipes. Many other herbs, of course, will reward your effort by enhancing your cooking and all are easy to grow.

Some herbs are annuals which means they grow in one season, and must be re-planted for the next year. But others are perennials; they will continue to grow each year without re-planting. Some perennial herbs — rosemary is one — are sensitive to extreme winter cold, and may not survive cold weather in the north.

Annual Herbs

Basil: Basil is available in several varieties with green leaves of different sizes, and one variety, Dark Opal, that has purple leaves. All have a similar flavor and will produce spikes with small purple or white flowers.

Basil seeds should be sowed ¼ inch deep and 2 to 3 inches apart after the last frost in the spring. When the seedlings are 3 inches high, thin until the plants are 12 inches apart. (Thinnings of all herbs can be used in cooking.) When the plant gets to be 4 inches high, leaves may be picked for using fresh. If allowed to grow, basil will become a 15 to 24-inch bush.

Basil can be started indoors about two months before the last frost is due. Plant in peat pots and later move pot and all into the garden, spacing the plants 12 inches apart.

Dill: Dill is cultivated for both its leaves and the seeds that form on the fan-shaped sprays of flowers that grow from the plant. Dill will grow to about 3 feet tall and can spread 3 feet wide. Try to plant dill in a place sheltered from the wind, to keep the seeds from blowing away, but remember that dill likes full sun too. Dill can be sown either in the spring or in the fall before the ground hardens with frost. Set the seeds about 2 to 3 inches apart, ¼ inch deep. When the seedlings have grown in the spring to about 2 inches high, thin so they stand 12 inches apart. Pick the leaves for use fresh at any time. Dill has a delicate taproot and does not transplant well so,

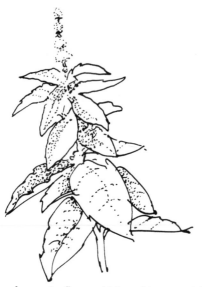

Basil has a sharp spicy flavor which combines especially well with tomatoes. It is a classic ingredient for spaghetti sauces. Both fresh and dry, it is good in hearty soups, stews and stuffing. Try with beans and fish, poultry, and pork dishes. Fresh basil is nice in salads.

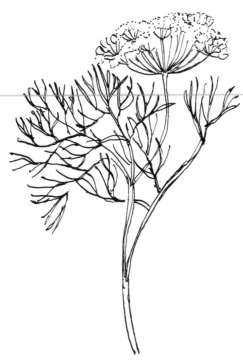

Dill has a cool, springlike flavor. Sprinkle fresh leaves on potato salads, cooked potatoes, sliced tomatoes and cucumbers, marinated navy beans and other vegetables. Chicken and seafood, especially salmon, are enhanced with dill. Dill and other herbs can be mixed with softened butter to make herb butter. Spread on slices of bread loaf, tie loaf together with string and heat in 300°oven.

if you grow dill indoors before the last frost, be sure to use a peat pot and transplant into the garden pot and all. Dill grows so quickly, you may want to make successive plantings every three or four weeks for a constant supply of the most abundant, young foliage.

Parsley: Parsley is properly a biennial, which means that it comes to maturity and blooms in the second year after it is planted. For the home garden, however, parsley is treated as an annual, and planted anew each year.

Parsley comes in many varieties, but the two best-known are French and Italian. French is the kind with the little curly leaves; most often found in the supermarket. Italian has larger, flat, deeper green leaves, and a more distinct flavor.

Sow parsley seeds after the last frost or just before the ground freezes in late fall. Parsley takes a long time to germinate; you can hurry the process by soaking the seeds in water for 24 hours before planting. When the seedlings are 2 to 3 inches tall, thin to 8 inches apart. Parsley can be started in pots before the last frost.

Perennial Herbs

Perennials don't grow as strongly as the annuals in their first year. Grow some perennial plants for harvesting the first year, and some others to leave alone so they will produce large strong plants the second year.

Chives: Chives are members of the onion family grown for their hollow, grass-like leaves. Chives grow 8 to 12 inches high and will eventually produce lovely purple flowers. (Don't look for these on plants grown in pots inside the house.) Chives can be grown from seed or by purchasing small plants at nurseries and supermarkets in the spring. If you plant seeds, sow ¼ inch deep and let grow into tight clumps. The thinnings are fresh chives. The more you thin, the more the plant will grow. Every few years, chives will pack their roots too tightly together and must be divided. Dig up the plant, cut up the root ball with a knife, throw out the center portion and transplant outer portions as 4-inch clumps about a foot apart.

Parsley combines well with many other herbs. Use chopped parsley fresh with potatoes and other vegetables, in gravies and sauces, on meat, and in egg dishes. When you cook parsley with dishes like stew, soup and casseroles, frozen parsley is fine. To freeze, wash, dry and pack whole or chopped sprigs in plastic bags.

Chives have a mild onion-like flavor. Cut fresh, for salads and garnishes. Use chives in cheese sauces, green sauces, and gravies. Sprinkle on cold soups, particularly vichyssoise and jellied consomme, and in chicken, seafood and egg dishes. Try chives mixed with sour cream, on baked potatoes. Freeze like parsley to preserve.

The Fruits And Vegetables   79

The distinctive flavor of mint goes well with sweet foods. Mint is traditional with lamb; combine with apple or currant jelly. Sprinkle mint on top of cooked peas and carrots just before serving. Use as a garnish on fruit salads, ice cream, and iced drinks. To make mint and other herb teas, use 2 teaspoons fresh leaves or 1 teaspoon dry leaves for each cup of boiling water.

Rosemary's sharp piny flavor goes especially well with lamb. Sprinkle on roast beef, pork, and veal. Add fresh leaves to marinades, and sparingly to meatloaf and sausage. Rosemary butter can be brushed on grilled fish or chicken.

Oregano is a highly aromatic, somewhat minty herb. Oregano, fresh or dried, goes well with sausage, meats, poultry and game, and is excellent in stuffings. Oregano is a necessity for pizza and enhances tomato dishes and spaghetti sauces. A little sprinkle of oregano is a splendid addition to summer squash, zucchini, eggplant and mushrooms.

The dry, savory flavor of sage is excellent for rich, fatty meats like pork, sausage, goose, rabbit. and duck. Fresh sage has a more delicate flavor than the dried leaf, and makes a good herb butter or flavoring for stuffings, wheat or bran dishes.

Mint: Mint comes in many different varieties — orange mint, apple mint, peppermint, and spearmint are just a few. Mints do not grow readily from seed; it is easier to buy root cuttings or young plants. Plant them early in the spring about 12 inches apart. Because the mint spreads quickly, your mint bed should be trimmed back frequently by hoeing deeply around its edges to uproot plants. For better control, plant mint in a large pot sunk in the ground, or sink a 10-inch strip of tar paper around the perimeter of the mint bed. Mint roots should be divided every third spring and reset 12 inches apart. Mint does best with frequent watering.

Rosemary: Rosemary is an evergreen shrub grown for its aromatic needle-like leaves. The plant wears violet-blue flowers. Rosemary needs full sun and can be grown from seeds, but the plants need two to three years to mature. It is easier to buy young plants or propagate from cuttings. Bring rosemary indoors for the winter where temperatures fall below 10°.

Oregano: Oregano is a perennial that is closely related to marjoram, and is grown for its tangy leaves. It can be substituted for thyme in recipes, but was chosen in preference to thyme here because it is a much prettier plant. Oregano can be grown from seed after the ground is well warmed in the spring, but is also available as young plants. Several slightly different plants are sold as oregano. All will give a somewhat similar taste to your cooking. But check the seed packet or nursery for differing cultivation requirements and hardiness. Plant oregano in the sunniest part of your garden, ¼ inch deep and 3 inches apart. When seedlings reach 3 inches high, thin the plants to 10 to 12 inches apart. It is easy to start oregano seeds indoors in a warm place and then transplant after the soil is warm.

Sage: Sage is a perennial grown for its aromatic leaves. The plants have small lilac-blue flowers that attract bees. You can get the dwarf sage variety which will be easier to care for. Sage can be grown from seeds sown ¼ inch deep in the spring but usually needs two years to reach a cuttable size. Young plants are available at nurseries. Thin sage until it is 10 to 16 inches apart. Or you can buy young plants and set them about 12 inches apart for the dwarf variety, 24 inches apart for the large plants. For strong new growth each year, cut back the previous year's plant by half each spring.

Tarragon: Tarragon is a 2 to 2½-foot bush grown for its licorice-tasting leaves. There are two kinds of tarragon: French and Russian. The French variety has more flavor but it produces sterile seeds and must be propagated from cuttings. If you see tarragon seed for sale, it is the Russian variety. The French variety is sold as young plants. Plant tarragon 2 feet apart in the early spring. When the plant is 6 inches high, you can begin snipping the branch tips from the top. This helps keep the plant bushy and neat. Tarragon plants should be divided and reset every third spring.

Drying Herbs

To dry herbs, harvest the leafy stems after flower buds have formed but before the plant blooms. At that time the leaves will have maximum flavoring oils in them. Cut off the stems leaving two sets of leaves at the base of each stem on the plant to allow it to continue growing. Wash the stems, and tie them in small bunches. Hang them upside down to dry in an airy, dry, shady place. Leave them for two weeks or until the leaves shrivel and dry. Then put the stems in a bowl and remove and discard as many bits of stems as you can. Put the leaves on a cookie sheet and put them in an oven set to its lowest heat. Heat them until the leaves are so dry that they crumble when rubbed. Pack the leaves in glass bottles or jars with airtight lids.

Potpourri

To make potpourri for scenting drawers and closets, combine whole spices like cloves and cinnamon sticks with dried herb leaves to get an aroma you like. Add dried wild rose petals, bayberries or other aromatic leaves and flowers that grow near you. Sprinkle with powdered orris root (available at pharmacies) to "fix" the aroma, and seal tightly in glass jars until you wish to use.

Tarragon has a slightly licorice flavor, which is classic for chicken. Crush whole fresh leaves to flavor marinades, Bernaise and mustard sauces. Try on egg, mushroom and tomato dishes. To make tarragon vinegar heat a pint of cider vinegar to boiling, put a sprig in a jar and pour the hot vinegar over it.

For convenience in wintering herbs indoors, plant in clay pots. "Plunge" the pots for the summer by burying them in the garden so that just the rim of the pot is above the surface of the garden. Dig up the pots in the fall and bring them indoors for the winter. This method gives herbs the benefit of outdoor light and air and a cool, moist soil during the summer months.

Perennial herbs that have been planted directly in the garden can be potted and brought indoors for the winter too. Annuals should be started afresh in pots indoors in early fall. The potted herbs will still need plenty of sunshine all winter.

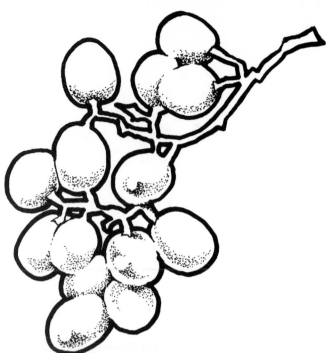

Recommended grape varieties are all descended from the wild Fox grape. One or two-year-old plants are available from your nursery or mail-order house for between $2 and $3 apiece, except for the seedless varieties, which will cost about $4.

Grapes

There are three types of grapes grown in North America. One is the European wine type, for which the Latin name is *Vitis vinifera*. Another is the wild Muscadine (*Vitis rotundifolia*) now being bred for commercial use in the south. The third is the wild Fox Grape (*Vitis labrusca*) that English settlers found growing in the north, cheerfully surviving the cold winters that would kill most European grape varieties. Unless you live in California or one of its neighboring states (where European grape growing is possible), you can grow only the Fox Grape varieties.

Grape Varieties

The unfussy Concord grape will succeed in a greater range of soils and climatic conditions than any other variety of American grape. It is the dark grape almost always used for grape juice, jelly and preserves. It makes a nice homemade red wine.

Buffalo is a dark purple grape grown for table use. It is valuable for those who want an early crop.

Catawba is a late-ripening red grape. It is regarded as better than Concord for wine-making.

Steuben is a dark grape that matures a little after Concord. It has a sharper, tangy taste. For making a wine that has an unusually good taste, try the Steuben.

Niagara is the leading American-type white grape. It can be used for wine or as a table grape.

Interlaken is a white grape especially good for very cold climates. Both Interlaken and Concord are also available in seedless varieties.

Grape Cultivation

Grapes are somewhat finicky about where they will grow. The top or side of a hill where the vine will be exposed to full sun and get good drainage is best. Avoid planting grapevines in "frost pockets," or low hollows that are not exposed to wind. It is possible to grow grape vines on many types of structures — fences, trellises, grape arbors. Since a vine lasts a long time, it will eventually cover the structure. If you have a bare wall that is exposed to full sun all day long, you can grow grapevines there, training them to climb the wall. The extra heat from the wall will hasten harvest time.

Leave 9 to 10 feet of space between each grapevine when you plant. Dig a hole big enough to accommodate the roots without crowding them. Put the plant in, and fill the hole, making sure the soil fills in tightly, leaving no air spaces. Tamp the soil down firmly with your foot. Don't expect a crop of grapes the first season, but unpruned vines may produce the following summer, and pruned vines will produce a superior crop in the third year. Many people don't bother to prune the grapevine until it has obviously grown too big for its support. Cared for in this way, vines will still produce grapes and be a decorative addition to your garden.

For best results, however, both in the size and quality of grapes produced and in the strength of the grapevine itself, it is a good idea to prune the grapevine. The usual method is called the four-arm Kniffen system, detailed on the next page.

As to fertilizer, the grapevines' greatest demand is that the soil be friable enough to drain well. It helps to dig in a few handfuls of an organic fertilizer like dried manure every few years, but it is not a must.

To make grape jam, pick off the stems of 2 quarts of Concord grapes. Squeeze out the pulp and save. Cook the skins gently for 15 to 20 minutes in ½ cup of water. Cook the pulp without water until soft; press the cooked pulp through a sieve or food mill to remove seeds.

Combine the pulp and skins with 6 cups sugar. Bring the mixture slowly to a boil, stirring until the sugar dissolves. Cook rapidly almost until the jelly point (216° to 220° on a candy thermometer). Stir frequently to prevent the mixture from sticking. Pour boiling hot into canning jars and seal. Process in boiling water-bath for 15 minutes.

Homemade wine requires no special equipment beyond a potato masher, a large open crock covered with window screen, gallon jugs, rubber stoppers with holes in them and plastic tubing (both of the latter items available at pet stores). Simple instructions are available at nominal cost from most agricultural colleges, or if you wish, a home wine-making kit can be purchased from most large department stores. A bushel of grapes makes 3 gallons of wine.

Grape Training

Grapevines trained by the Kniffen system will continue to produce for many years. After about 15 years, you can leave unpruned one of the "sucker" vines that grows from the base of the stem. Tie this up at the end of the following season, just as you did your original stem, and at the end of the next season, prune the old main stem and use the new stem as the main part of the plant.

The First Year

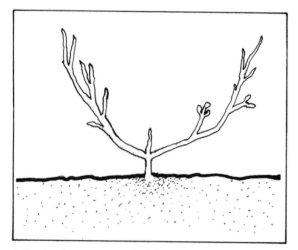

1. The newly transplanted vine will look something like this.

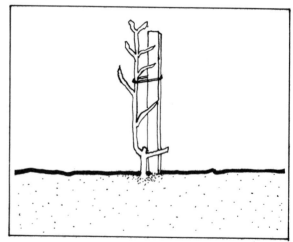

2. After planting in the spring, snip off the top of the vine with a hand-pruner so that only two buds are above ground.

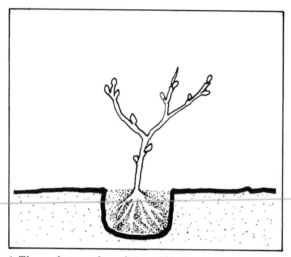

3. During the summer, each of the two buds you left will form a side branch.

4. In the fall, select the stronger branch. Stake it upright. Cut off the weaker branch.

The Second Year

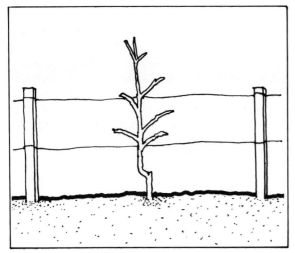

1. Build a fence of two wires (2 and 4 feet from the ground) to train your vines along. Allow 7 to 8 feet of wire on either side of each plant, as the total spread of a vine will be 15 feet.

2. As the side branches grow from the single stem during the summer, select the four strongest ones and tie them along the wires. Snip off all but four of the remaining branches. Prune these four back to two buds each.

The Third Year

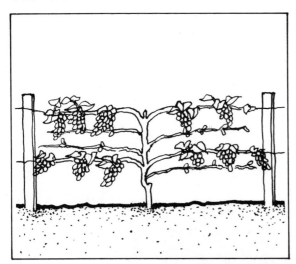

1. The four branches tied to the wires during the previous year will produce grapes this year. Meanwhile, the four stubs you left on will be growing branches that will produce the following year. They can be left hanging through the summer.

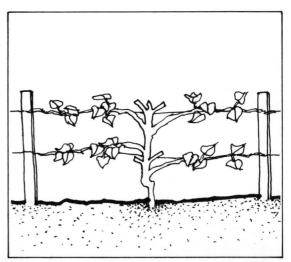

2. After harvest cut off the four branches that have produced grapes, tie up the four strongest of the new branches that grew from the stubs, and again cut off all other branches, leaving only four double-budded stubs for new growth next summer. The same process is now repeated annually.

Dwarf Apples And Pears

Dwarf fruit trees are much smaller than regular fruit trees, yet the fruit that grows on dwarf trees is full-sized. Dwarf fruit trees produce fruit within two years after transplanting — long before regular-size trees reach maturity. You can harvest most of the fruit without a ladder.

The most successful dwarf trees have been apples and pears. Dwarf peaches and plums are available, but they are not much smaller than the regular-size trees. For the small garden, apples and pears are the best choice.

If you decide to try planting dwarf trees, keep in mind that apples need other varieties of the same fruit nearby for good pollination. A neighbor's apple tree will be sufficient to pollinate your dwarf apple, but if you have no fruit trees growing nearby, you must purchase and plant at least two varieties of apple. Your nurseryman will advise you on which varieties he has that are most effective in pollinating others.

Dwarf Apple And Pear Cultivation

Apples and pears can be transplanted spring or fall. A two-year-old tree will cost about $10. Select a tree with a strong trunk and good branching. Plant it as soon as you bring it home from the nursery. If you are planting several trees, place them at least 12 feet apart.

Dig a hole wider and deeper than the root ball. Place the tree gently in the hole. Dwarf trees are produced by grafting full-size trees onto dwarf roots. The place where the graft was

Gnawing animals can attack the tender bark of your fruit trees during their first few seasons. To guard against rabbits and field mice wrap a cylinder of hardware cloth around the bottom 2 feet of trunk.

McIntosh has the best reputation as an all-purpose red apple, excellent both for eating and cooking. It also stores well.

Rome apples, deepest red, large and juicy, make the perfect baked apple.

Yellow Delicious and Richard (Red) Delicious are crisp and juicy apples, known for their fragrance and used as a dessert fruit.

Baldwin, a yellow apple with some red color, is also crisp and juicy. It is a particularly good keeper.

Greenings are the classic green pie apple, valued for their tartness.

made shows clearly as a bulge. This bulge must be above the surface of the soil. If it is not, the portion of the trunk above the graft will send out roots and you will have lost the dwarf quality of your tree. Check the level of the graft before you fill the hole, and if necessary add more soil to the bottom of the hole to raise the tree higher. When the level is correct, pack good topsoil around the root system. If you have a heavy clay soil, the use of wet peat moss mixed with the soil can stimulate tree growth. The soil should be moist but not water-logged. Pack the soil closely around the roots with your fingers so there is complete contact between the root and the soil. Tamp down tightly, adding soil to bring the ground up to level. Fertilizer is not needed at planting time, and probably will not ever be needed.

Cultivate the ground around your young tree thoroughly in the early summer. It is important that the soil remain loose above the root system so you will get good drainage.

Fruit trees will rarely require watering except in a drought. Then one watering once a week at night with a repeat watering the next morning will be sufficient. Too much water can harm the root system of your tree and may prevent it from bearing fruit.

When fruit comes, you will have to do some thinning. Most fruit trees provide an abundance of fruit that the tree cannot support. Pick off some of the young fruit before it matures, leaving a space between the remaining fruit of 4 to 5 inches.

When you plant your young tree you will probably need to tie it to supports, since the dwarf root-stock does not provide very firm anchorage while young. Iron pipes or wooden stakes can be used for support. A single tie with good grade clothesline about 2 or 3 feet above the ground will be adequate for a newly planted tree.

Bosc is a russet-colored pear, resistant to flaws and very juicy.

Seckel is a small pear, frequently used for preserving as spiced pears because of its firm texture and small size.

Bartlett is a large, thin-skinned, especially fragrant pear; golden yellow with a blush of red when fully ripe.

Angouleme is a huge fruit with unusual butter-colored flesh.

Pruning And Training Dwarf Fruit Trees

Dwarf fruit trees will need pruning to maintain their vigor and continue fruit bearing. Pruning requires the understanding of a few basic principles, common sense, and good pruning tools.

A dwarf tree can be pruned to its natural shape, or trained to a flat space-saving shape against a fence or wall. The flat method is called espalier. Such trees produce very well. Long-handled pruning shears are needed for naturally shaped trees. Hand pruners may be all you need for espalier pruning.

Pruning To A Natural Shape

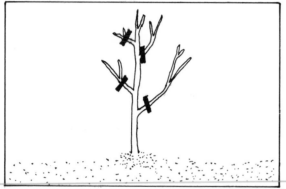

The transplanted baby tree is usually cut back to 3 to 5 branches when it is first planted. The place in the trunk where it was grafted should be at least 2 inches above ground.

Each spring, clip off branches that grow back toward the center of the tree, branches that have grown excessively longer than their neighbors, and branches that cross one another. Suckers may sprout from the base of the tree. Cut them off, leaving no stubs.

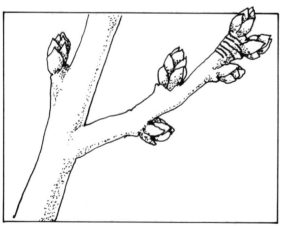

The fruit of both apples and pears grows from "spurs" – short, thick branches that never grow long. Be sure not to prune them off by mistake. If a spur carries several fruits, pluck a few off while very young, leaving fruits 4 inches apart so each can grow to full size.

As the tree grows older, there may be dead or diseased branches which should be removed flush with the trunk. Annual care will result in well-spaced branching, allowing plenty of sun and air to reach the developing fruit.

Training To Espalier

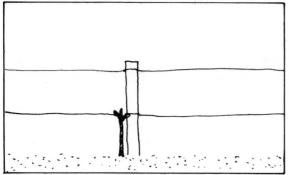

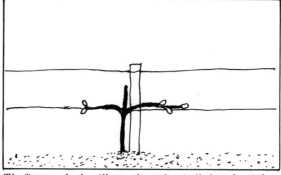

Espaliered trees are shaped to grow two-dimensionally against a flat surface, like a wall or fence. To make the simplest espalier, a double cordon, begin by pruning all but two buds or branches on opposites of the trunk and suitably close together.

The first two buds will grow branches (called cordons) that should be trained horizontally. Tie the branches to wires strung between stakes, or use pruning nails to hold them against a fence or house wall. Don't be afraid to bend young branches – they are very supple.

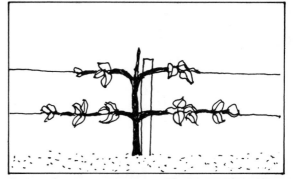

About 18 inches above the first set of branches, choose another pair of buds or young branches to train horizontally. They will be trained in the same way as the first two. Meanwhile, all extra branches should be pruned off at the trunk to allow maximum growth of the preferred cordon branches.

To keep the pattern clear, prune off all vertical branches along the horizontal ones. Cut close to the branch, not leaving a stub. Stubs will heal less readily than the main stem will. Use a hand pruner or fingernails if you can catch the branch while it is only a bud.

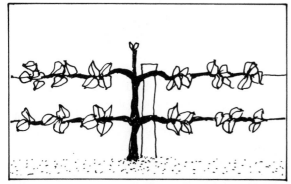

Established branches will continue to grow longer. As they grow, they can be tied along their support with cotton twine, jute garden cord, or raffia; or nailed with espalier nails. Allow room for the branch to get thicker too. Tying should be done constantly for a clean job of training.

If you want to stop the vertical growth of the tree now, cut off the leader (main stem) at the point where the second set of branches grows. This is a double cordon pattern. If you want the tree taller, continue to choose pairs of buds every 18 inches and train the branches horizontally.

Apple Recipes

Apple Conserves

Fruit conserves are jam-like products that are made by cooking two or more fruits with sugar until thick enough to congeal on a spoon. Conserves can be spread on bread, or used as a dessert topping. Many are made with citrus fruits, nuts and raisins. Here is a recipe for one kind:

1 quart chopped, cored, pared tart apples
1 quart stemmed berries or other fruit, peeled
6 cups sugar   ½ cup seedless raisins
¼ cup lemon juice   ½ cup chopped walnuts

Combine all the ingredients except the nuts and cook slowly until the sugar dissolves. Then boil rapidly until the mixture is thick. Stir to prevent sticking. This will take about 20 minutes. In the last 5 minutes add the chopped nuts. Pour the boiling conserves into sterilized canning jars. Cover and process in a hot water-bath at 180°-185° for 15 minutes. (The hot water-bath is the same as a boiling water-bath, but the water is kept at a lower temperature. Use a thermometer, and adjust the flame or burner of your stove so that the temperature stays at 180°-185°.)

Apple Jelly

Jelly is made by cooking fruit juice with sugar. The end product should be firm enough to hold its shape and soft enough to spread with a knife. Many fruits do not contain enough natural pectin to make jelly. For these, buy commercially-prepared pectin and add it according to the instructions on the package. Apple, quince and grape jelly can be made without commercial pectin.

It is easiest to make jelly in small quantities, using no more than 6 cups of juice at a time. Use tart apples; make sure about a quarter of them are slightly underripe. Wash the apples, removing stems and blossom ends. Do not core or peel. Cut the apples into small pieces and add water to cover. Bring the mixture quickly to a boil. Reduce heat and simmer 25 minutes, until the apples are soft. Now extract the juice by pouring the mixture through a jelly bag or cheesecloth bag.

Juice for jelly is strained to make it clear. The juice may take overnight to strain through the cloth. A jelly bag is usually made of muslin, shaped like a long cone so the juice drips from the point. It must be hung over a bowl. If this seems too complicated, you could simply drape a piece of muslin over a colander on top of the bowl to catch the juice as it drips through the cloth. If you are in a hurry, use cheesecloth or a fine strainer. The jelly will not be crystal clear, but it will taste just as good.

Measure the apple juice into a kettle. Add 3 cups of sugar for every 4 cups of apple juice. Boil over high heat, stirring until the mixture reaches 220°. Use a candy thermometer. The jelly is ready when it breaks from the spoon in a sheet. Remove from stove and skim off foam.

Fill jelly glasses with the mixture to within ½ inch of the top. Cover immediately with ⅛-inch layer of hot but not smoking paraffin, heated in the top half of a double boiler. Allow jars to stand until paraffin is hard. Cover with lids.

Pear Recipes

Spiced Pears

8 pounds Seckel pears	10 cups sugar
8 cinnamon sticks	2 cups water
2 tablespoons whole cloves	4 cups cider vinegar

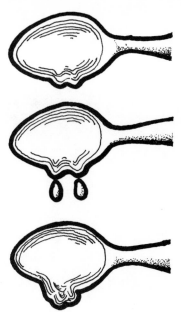

You can tell when a liquid is ready to jell by the way it drips from a spoon. At first, the jelly is just a thin liquid. As it thickens, heavier drops form, but still drip from the spoon separately. When the jelly is ready (216° to 220° on a candy thermometer) two drops will fall from the spoon separately but instead form into one drop and break from the spoon in a sheet, or flake. If you blow on the spoon to cool it, the syrup will now jell.

Wash the pears, remove the blossom end and peel, but leave the stem in place. Stud each pear with 4 whole cloves. Mix together with the water, vinegar and sugar in a large saucepan, and heat until the sugar dissolves. Add the cinnamon sticks and clove-studded pears, and boil until the pears are tender — about 15 minutes. Pack the pears in sterilized canning jars, adding a cinnamon stick to each jar. Reheat the syrup to a boil, and pour the syrup over the pears, filling the jars to the top. Seal at once. Yield: about 8 pints.

Pear Butter

Fruit butters are made by cooking fruit pulp with sugar to a thick enough consistency for spreading. Peel pears, remove blossom ends and stems, quarter but do not core. Cook in a small quantity of water until mushy. Put the pulp through a food mill and measure it. Add sugar in the ratio of 2 cups for each quart of pulp. Add a teaspoon of ground cinnamon and a pinch of clove for each quart if you like a spicy butter, or season to taste with allspice, nutmeg or mace. Cook the mixture, stirring very frequently on the lowest heat, using an asbestos pad to reduce the heat if necessary. Cook until the butter is thick enough to spread. Pour into sterilized jars, leaving ¼-inch headspace, and process in hot water-bath (180°-185°) for 10 minutes.

Fruit jams are made by cooking crushed or chopped fruits with sugar until the mixture will round up on a spoon. Two quarts of fruit will need about 6 cups of sugar for jam. Peel, pit and crush the fruit. Add ½ cup water and cook gently for 10 minutes. Add sugar, boil gently until thick, stirring frequently. Pour boiling hot into sterilized jars. Process for 15 minutes in boiling water-bath.

Index